TALES
OF
MODERN DAY
MOUNTAIN MEN

HELPING TEENS DISCOVER BALANCE
AND RENEWAL THROUGH NATURE

RON SMITH

DEDICATION

To Bob Meyer, "The Austin Mountain Man."
From countless Mountain Men across fifty-seven years of adventures, it is with deepest affection, gratitude and respect that this book is dedicated to you.

TABLE OF CONTENTS

FINDING THE RIGHT TRAIL

Daily, each of us gets to choose from many possible paths. What is critical for people today has been critical for thousands of years. Namely, we need to be aware of God's influence in our daily life and his desires for us. God works with us and through us more often than we take time to consider. If you look around, you will discover a myriad of opportunities to encourage others. Likewise, if you are receptive, you will find that others are there and ready to encourage you. In either case, there are daily opportunities to build successful relationships. I am amazed at the people I have met in my lifetime, people much stronger, wiser and more accomplished than I, yet talking with me, encouraging me to use my gifts and talents to help others use theirs!

These are people who have reached a maturity level where they understand that life is not about them but about helping others. This awareness comes sooner for some than others, but with pursuit, it can come to all.

God wants us to make a positive difference every day in the lives we encounter. While often easier said than done, given our own struggles and selfishness, there are always opportunities—if we so choose. To be selfless, we must make a daily decision to overcome whatever may arise. It is not uncommon for our attitude and perspective to become twisted as a result of misalignment in our life. This misalignment can then prevent us from making selfless, daily decisions within the context of our behavior because we are preoccupied with our own problems, thoughts, issues, etc.

Let me explain what I mean by alignment and misalignment. Over the years I have observed that if people can accurately define and line up three critical factors—their passions, their skills and their abilities, along with a commitment to serve others—then they will be living life within what many commonly call "the will of God." Many times success comes to people after long struggles trying be something they are not. This transformation usually happens when they have made decisions that finally provide them opportunities to align their passions with their skills and abilities.

As an educator and camp leader, one of the most important things I try to do is to help young people identify, understand and align these critical life factors. My hope is to empower kids to make good choices and ultimately, gain lifelong satisfaction through alignment. Finding alignment is challenging for anyone, but particularly for adolescents and young adults given the emphasis on the technology economy. According to a 2010 survey by Mercer, a global HR consultancy firm, 32 percent of U.S. workers were seriously considering leaving their jobs due to dissatisfaction. But the percentage increased to 40 percent for workers aged 25 to 34 and 44 percent for workers under the age of 24. This sounds like misalignment to me.

Today it is not unusual to hear people say, "I only work to pay the bills! If I could only win the lottery, I would be all set!" If you look closely you will find that these folks are often misaligned in their work choices. It is important to realize that God wired us to work. We were not designed to win the lottery and retire from the world. Work is good! Without work, we often fall apart. People need and want meaningful work. Take a look at some of our most celebrated people: actors, athletes and musicians. Many have buckets of money, superior talent, noteriety and time galore. Oddly, even with seemingly limitless resources, a good many fall into states of negative mental health.

On a more ordinary level, consider our society in general. According to a survey by the National Institute on Drug Abuse, in 2009, the United States achieved first place among seventeen nations surveyed in the use and abuse of cocaine, cannabis and tobacco. We ranked sixth in alcohol abuse. With recent trends to legalize cannabis who really knows what long-term societal results may develop? We do know this much for sure; most drug, alcohol and tobacco abuse starts in adolescence.

Why does all this self-abuse appear so early in life? I'd venture that a young person's misalignment of abilities, passions and skills combined with a lack of spiritual leadership hinders the development of his identity, positive self-esteem and confidence. Stated another way: now, more than ever, young people need help finding the right trails in life.

Consider a few conceptual examples of alignment and misalignment. Let's say a young person expresses a desire to work in the outdoors, but he has no ability to endure the actual discomforts of nature which results in a misalignment. Another alignment challenge involves a young man wanting to become a physician, but has limited abilities in mathematics and science. Although his passion may be great, he simply cannot study hard enough to earn grades to achieve his dream. These folks are misaligned in their approach to a vocation.

I often encountered examples of misalignment in my previous life. Formerly I was a human resources executive at Motorola, Cadence Design Systems and a couple of other premier American high-tech firms. I often traveled the world finding and hiring the brightest talent available and then worked with teams to integrate them into positions to create world-class technology solutions. One day I was at a major university interviewing graduating electrical engineering students and one student in particular presented a remarkable story. This man had already earned a Bachelor of Science degree, secured a spot in medical school and with hard work was awarded an M.D. degree. He then entered a residency program. Along the way he became disillusioned with medicine and quit the program.

During our interview I asked the obvious question, "After all the years of preparation, the dedication to study, the money, the time, why did you quit?"

"I did not like working with people," he replied. "I was more interested in the technology keeping people alive and helping them heal than I was in the day-to-day interaction with the people themselves." So back to university he went, earning an MS in electrical engineering. He became a star at our company and created many new, leading-edge electronic and medical product patents as a result of his vast knowledge. Simply stated, he became aligned.

While in high tech I was fortunate to have worked with some of the most creative minds in developing technology, ranging from the early Motorola "brick" cell phone creators to today's software driven

x

smart-phone geniuses. The companies I worked for were complex, sophisticated, global organizations. Yet I often noticed misalignment of work choices and placements among employees. I saw how misalignment produces conflict, pain, frustration, stress, depression and lack of productivity. Those results can lead to abuse of self and others, and can be very destructive to teams. Proper alignment though, produces amazing results: creativity, energy and endurance, laughter, joy, accomplishment, a peaceful spirit, a desire to help others, confidence and pride. In other words, alignment produces positive contributions to self, others and society. If we are truly aligned we are living out God's plan for our lives.

Let me share a very personal story concerning alignment. Consider September 11, 2001. You might be wondering, "What is the connection between 9/11 and alignment?" The terrorist attacks on the World Trade Center forever changed America and the world, and for many of us, it also brought our individual value systems under personal scrutiny. This was the same time when the dot.com rocket had reached its apogee and exploded. Huge financial losses in the market ensued along with massive unemployment. At this time I was deeply embedded in the field of high-technology human resources, but coupled with other considerations, 9/11 became a wake-up call. I needed better alignment in my own life.

I exited the high-tech world. After great mental struggle, I chose to build a youth-leadership, travel-adventure camp for boys and to teach science. Not exactly mainstream goals for my high-tech peers! In fact, many considered my plans ridiculous, but I wanted to consider this particular option for real. With much stress, effort, prayer and support, I took a huge leap of faith and created the Fort Smith Mountain Men Adventure Camp. The camp is based upon the famous

Meyer's Mountain Men camps I attended as a teenager, but now it also includes history, natural science and leadership training. Now a decade plus down the trail, and after working with hundreds of young Mountain Men, as we call our campers; the camp has proven to be amazing! We have helped many young people find themselves.

What I have learned in over a decade of time in the middle-school classroom and over thousands of miles on the trail is that it is especially difficult—and essential—for young men to discover alignment. I believe that now, in our increasingly secularized society glued together by always-on technology, they need intentional guidance and support from *everyone* in their lives, especially their parents. To grow into successful men of character, they must have role models and interested persons to guide them daily. Will they emerge from the cocoon of adolescence into capable and responsible men as God intended, or will they follow the increasingly common path of delayed adolescence and self-absorption into their late twenties, early thirties and beyond? The answer depends largely upon how much time, love and coaching we invest in our boys.

Tales of Modern Day Mountain Men can help guide you in this process. The book illustrates how young men need predictable, intentional daily training. It illuminates how they benefit from less technology, and more connection with the simple pleasures found in nature. Once a healthy dose of prayer is added in, you will see how this leads to discovering God's trail map for each of our lives. We just have to open it, read it, understand it and then align with that map for the benefit of ourselves, our youth and society.

THE TECHNOLOGY DILEMMA

K ids. They are a blessing from God. They are also a challenge. Boys in particular are a unique flavor of challenge tending toward the spicier end of the spectrum. Our society has evolved radically, putting them in a true bind. To name a few challenges they are facing:

The pressure to achieve academically has increased exponentially in the last twenty years—and is accelerating.

The amount and complexity of information and technology pushed on them is mind boggling. All of the time spent on testing and technology means that we may be skipping over basic cognitive learning and development capabilities by age, with kids missing out on very real emotional needs for play, for decompression and being outdoors. We are also beginning to notice that with our drive toward increasing rigor and measurement in education we are starting to see, in some cases, a student movement away from achievement and toward academic apathy. There is a notable increase in the levels of stress being seen in our kids as a result of higher and higher expectations for performance based upon testing. This emphasis on testing is, in some cases, causing severe anxiety in our kids and a subsequent lack of performance. Exactly the opposite of what we are trying to accomplish. Could it be that some of our kids are burning out on an education system based on testing? From my experience, there is no question that all kids can learn; however, we all learn in different ways and at different speeds. Given all the incredible shifts in society, our one-size fits all public program may be reaching its limits of properly fitting anyone. What we may need to consider now is how the system is designed and delivered. We need to look at what is most important for our kids to learn in order to help them develop into successful adults in our global society. What we might want to look at, in addition to academics, would be an emphasis on developing competencies like personal management and interpersonal skills. Perhaps we should direct more effort toward developing our kids' levels of emotional intelligence along with leadership and presentation skills. Surely competence in these critical skills will help them achieve more stability and success in whatever vocational choices and personal relationships may lie ahead. As we engage the development of these competencies, perhaps the single, most important investment we can make in our kids would be for us to help them identify who they really are. This can be done through helping them find their innate gifts and passions then coaching them to find alignment within the context of economic reality. Successfully done, this will help kids find their path into an enjoyable and productive life.

Another challenge to kids is the American divorce rate. While seemingly leveling off below a high around 50 percent (given the trend of more people living together or postponing marriage) the trend has still left the majority of our kids being raised in a blended family, single-parent, grandparent-parent, cohabitating or non-traditional home. Only 46% of our families are now considered to be two-parent, traditional family units. Moreover, two-income, more affluent households have everyone pursuing more stuff and influencing the lesser endowed homes to try and keep up as well. Stuff like big screen TV's with hundreds of virtually worthless channels and of course, more video games, some offering multiplayer global participation. And lest we forget, the latest smart phone upgrade with all the apps. Again, an overload of technology options....

The bottom line? Kids need help. They need dependable adult leadership. They need both a mother and a father in the home. They need role models and mentors. They need love, attention and guidance, not another video game, Xbox, smart phone, iPad application or more time wasted on social media. Consider that thought along with the media perspective recently provided by *Time* magazine, which chose to spotlight Facebook's founder, Mark Zuckerberg, on its December 2014 cover. The article estimated that 85 percent of humans are now living within range of a cell tower. What were Zuckerberg's thoughts on that statistic? Get the remaining fifteen percent online as fast as possible using satellites and other technology so everyone on the planet is connected! A really shocking reality is that, according to a 2013 article in the *Corvallis Advocate,* more people on the planet have access to cell phone technology than they do to clean, running water, indoor plumbing or electricity!

In an article in *The Wall Street Journal,* Christopher Mims comes up with a new expression for all this hyper-connectedness. According to Mims, the "distraction-industrial complex" is how technology is impacting our focus in life on all levels. Every trend in consumer technology—phones, video games, computers and other engrossing electronic devices—is geared toward even more frequent and effective interruptions aimed at gaining our attention, hence the distraction-industrial complex.

Take the concept of "push" technology. Instant notifications through Facebook, Twitter, Instagram and dozens of other applications have hooked people, youngsters especially, through a basic human emotional need for connectedness. According to a recent piece in *Computers and Human Behavior,* Internet Addiction has become recognized worldwide as a psychological disorder. Why? There are probably as many reasons as there are people out there but mostly because it offers immediate gratification. Whether used for research, curiosity or play, the Internet can be hugely addictive—and distracting—to lives.

We need to collectively weigh in now on what's really going on: technology is cool; there are marvelous applications in entertainment, medicine, manufacturing, commerce, education, exploration and yes, even communications, but at what cost to our productivity, our relationships and our mental health? After all, the thinking goes, if we don't keep up, we will be left behind. We will risk losing our "coolness factor." We soldier on. We text and talk. We text and drive. We echo trite expressions of justification: "It's just life in the fast lane," "Gotta get it while you can," "Time and no money, or money but no time," and a personal favorite of mine that has changed over time: "I still have quality time with my kids because of technology." Really?

Interestingly, the concept of "time poverty" has now entered our vernacular. Similar in concept to financial poverty—that being a condition of having too many bills or spending beyond the amount of our income—time poverty can be described as a condition that exists when there is simply too much going on to complete what needs to be done. The problem is deciding what needs to be accomplished versus what we think needs to be done. Prioritization confuses us: how do we allocate the limited number of minutes, hours and days of life to specific activities?

Time poverty explains our dilemma of working exhaustively to provide at a level we deem appropriate but then having too little time to enjoy the fruits of our labor. Or the dilemma of being too busy and too stressed or too tired to play! Our connectedness keeps us in the time sink loop: always on, always available and always expected to answer.

Consider time poverty in relation to communication and entertainment, which are of consuming interest to Americans. Recent studies by the Pew Research Center indicate that our youth, ages twelve to seventeen, are now texting at a median rate of 60 - 100 times per day; this is up from 50 times, in 2009. Texting now far surpasses all other forms of communication between teens. This includes talking by cell phone, face-to-face socializing, social-network messaging, instant messaging, talking on landlines and emailing! Astoundingly, three-quarters of teens in the United States now have cell phones. We have to ask ourselves where and on what are our kids spending their time?

Studies investigating the impacts of time poverty on society by Kirk Warren Brown and Richard M. Ryan of the University of Rochester suggest that rather than helping us accomplish more, this unrelenting press to always be connected, as well as our constant drive for money and prestige, are actually leading to cognitive overload... those feelings of stress and pressure that keep us from being in the moment.

It is critical for us to remember we are not one- and zero-based machines. We are humans. We are wired to require the experience of the ebb and flow of life through downtime, reflection and community. We need time to think! We need time to be in the moments of life....

In her recent book *Alone Together*, MIT's Sherry Turkle, a professor of Social Studies of Science and Technology, explains the results of her fifteen-year study on our lives within the digital terrain. Turkle unravels the mysteries we see being created through the use of technology on our privacy, community, intimacy and solitude. Her book title says it all: alone together. With research findings similar to Turkle, psychologist and author Hugh MacKay states that connection is the lifeblood of our society. Like Turkle he maintains that the hyper-connectedness we are experiencing through technology is really an illusion.

The grave paradox we must consider is this: are we exchanging face-to-face interaction for digital connection and yet thinking we are more connected? True, false or maybe? In a recent issue of *CIO Magazine*, Chuck Martin discusses the effectiveness in the use of technology in business communications. In the article, senior executives are beginning to lament the use and misuse of email, texting, etc. in the course of trying to manage organizational productivity and employee relations. For instance, email is cited as potentially delaying decision-making by passing the idea round and round, and creating a management environment of failure to act. Surprisingly, the article states that the majority of business leaders believe that the organizations would be more productive if people would utilize face-to-face communications first and only use technology as a backup. What an eye-opener: all agree there is no substitute for in-person communications.

Indeed today's glued-to-technology adults and kids are in some cases seemingly losing critical communication skills including spelling. Real communication involves many facets such as tone of voice, inflection, facial expression, body posture, movement and writing. I am aware of situations where teens are dating exclusively through texting and smart phone communications. I've watched kids bump into each other as they walk down school hallways and through shopping malls staring down at their cell phones, addicted to the stimulus of the next text, Tweet, or Instagram. I've seen families in restaurants staring at their phones and texting, no conversation, alone together. I've noticed a mom pushing her child on a swing set while talking on a cell phone; the kid is playing with the mom but the mom is not playing with the kid, although she thinks she is. And I've seen parents working non-stop on a computer at home while their children play on their own digital baby-sitting technologies—everyone together, but frustratingly apart.

Try this little experiment. The next time you pull up to a traffic light, look over into the car next to you. Chances are good that you will witness people texting on smart phones. I can almost guarantee that if you drive around the high-tech megalopolis of Austin, near where I live, and travel on the Capital of Texas Highway, you will be shocked at the number of people texting while whizzing by at high speeds. It seems today to be standard practice. After all, we have to be in touch! In point of fact, use of hand-held, mobile devices including texting in cars, has become so bad that Austin recently passed an ordinance prohibiting texting and driving.

However we got here the symptoms are becoming clear. We are too busy and too self-focused for our own good. Jean M. Twenge, a sociologist looking at generational change in America, offers up compelling observations in her book, *The Narcissism Epidemic*. Our society, she observes, has become so enthralled with itself and starved for recognition and connection that it is threatening us and our youth from within. Dr. Twenge, along with others, makes uncomfortable yet verifiable observations about the dark side of technology and how it is negatively affecting our young people, their emotional growth and their overall mental health. No surprise then, what needs to be done involves managing our use of technology.

So where are authorities pointing for solutions? Richard Louv, author of *Last Child in the Woods* and *The Nature Principle*, writes thought-provokingly about how children are suffering from what he calls "nature deficit disorder." People need to be outdoors in nature! Through research-based examples, Louv explains the many negative impacts children suffer as a result of an always-on society and the lack of connectedness with nature. His research proves that direct exposure to nature is essential for emotional and physical health for both children and adults; he gives examples of successful, nature-based remedies.

As we consider what else is good (and not so good) for raising kids and what helps to build strong character and emotional stability, researchers are sharing other excellent insights. Dr. Brene Brown, a research professor at the University of Houston Graduate College of Social Work, eloquently articulates how to develop and maintain positive mental health. In her work she notes that the root components required for solid, emotional, mental health include courage, compassion, connections and vulnerability—with the most important component being connections. This basic human need then clearly explains the rapid and widespread proliferation of social media. Paul Tough in *How Children Succeed* outlines many positive ideas that bring hope and ideas to parents raising children. His research is not about academic achievement. Rather, he suggests, what really produces that sense of lifelong well-being are qualities such as character, determination, grit and curiosity. The question for us then, is how do we develop these qualities in our kids?

Among the very successful, research-based and field-tested approaches for consideration is that of Dr. John Trent, Chair of Marriage and Family at Moody Theological Seminary and President of StrongFamiles.com. Through his work, Dr. Trent is a leading proponent of developing and nurturing families and churches through "deliberate intent." His approach which he calls, *"The Blessing Challenge,"* seeks to produce successful, godly people by understanding and delivering God's intent of blessing for those in our lives. His work also includes ground-breaking cooperative efforts with partners like Kurt Bruner and Steve Stroope of Lake Pointe Church; their team in concert with Dr. James Dobson's, Focus on the Family, and others pioneered the innovative strategies of HomePointe, Inc. The solutions provided through HomePointe focus on parents and influential family members creating a culture of deliberate and focused efforts directed at developing spiritual understanding and character in the home. Families are equipped with resources to begin first at home within marriage and then into the extended family, followed by the church, friendships and the workplace. Thus, the family becomes the core unit for training and support, as intended, so that the moral, spiritual and social concepts God gave us can be nurtured and grown, preparing us to serve others.

In your quest to find useful answers on raising boys you have picked up this book. Like me, you know that life is too fast for them. Honestly, you might agree, that most of the time it is too fast for us adults! You see how life is cluttered with stuff and technological distractions. You sense that a severe shortage of quiet time destabilizes them, creating anxiety and contributing to an inability to focus. Fortunately in my work with thousands of young people during the past thirteen years, I have been able to come up with some proven ways to help them—and now you and your boys. Soon you will learn how to block out, at least temporarily, the negative noise of life and help them develop depth of character, positive-thinking skills and deeper spiritual beliefs. There are ways to move toward a more practical, more mindful balance of technology use in their lives. Your boys will have a better opportunity to become aligned with their true purpose in life.

So, what can you do right now, today? Read on....

Tales of Modern Day Mountain Men is intended to provide opportunity for thought and introspection. The following fifteen, rain-and-mud-real stories are of boys playing, laughing and learning in the outdoors. Enjoy each story and at the end of the chapter—in the reflection about "Building Young Men" and the nuggets of hands-on advice in "Consider the Boys in Your Life"—take some notes and then try out these ideas with your young men. As you will see, the key methodology I use for reaching the real kid inside is through accessing the beauty of God's handiwork in nature while applying some tried-and-true leadership skills. This is what boys can look like when not enveloped in a bubble of technology. So join us as we travel together on the open road, across the beautiful continent of North America and all the way up into Alaska. No close calls with bears or moose for you. No mosquito bites either. From a "50,000-foot view," safe and dry, you will become familiar with my common-sense concepts and techniques and see how you can use these practices to transform lives within your circle.

Most importantly, within these times of high-speed life challenges, my message to you is one of hope. What a joy to have boys in your life!

Fishing the Colorado

La Grange, Texas, May 1942

"A boy's will is the wind's will, and the thoughts of youth are long, long thoughts."

— Henry Wadsworth Longfellow

A slight breeze blew gently through the opened windows of the small schoolhouse. Outside the day was opening up to be a special day. The sky was magically clear, painted the sharpest and deepest of blended blues and accented by a few soft, billowy cumulus clouds floating lazily above stately pecan trees. In a tree limb near the windows, a mockingbird sang out with authority. Announcing to all who would listen, this was, in fact, a special day.

Transfixed by the moment, a young boy in the schoolroom gazed out the window. Then he looked to the front of the room at the teacher who was writing the day's lessons on the chalkboard. His mind and eyes wandered back to the window where the mockingbird continued to advertise the day's beginning. As he stared out the window he absentmindedly raised his hand.

"Yes, Bobby?"

"I need to go, Miss Hoyt."

"Do you need to use the restroom?" she asked. "If so, come right back—okay? We need to get started."

"Yes ma'am," he replied.

Due to his previous lack of academic attention, Bobby had earned a front-row seat just off to the right of Miss Hoyt's desk. He got up and made his way down the middle aisle toward the open door. As he passed by his buddy Jimmy, he gave a quick wink. Jimmy smiled, shook his head and looked down. Bobby then headed toward the restroom. His heart beating rapidly, he looked up and down the hallway. The coast was clear, at least for now. Bobby strode briskly out the door. Adrenalin spurred him to run as fast as he could away from school.

Every boy knows this feeling of running as fast as possible but feeling like your feet are stuck in mud and that you will be caught at any moment for whatever transgression or monster you are fleeing. Faster and faster he ran. Out across the football field, down the hill and toward the river. Once safely over the hill, he began laughing out loud. "Yippee! What a day!" he yelled out. Cheerful, whistling and without a care, he headed to Cedar Creek, a small tributary cut into the banks of the Colorado River. Bobby and his family knew Mr. Johnson, the landowner of Cedar Creek. He had fished there many times with his daddy so he was certain it would be okay to fish today.

For his latest adventure, Bobby knew he would pay a steep price at home with his parents later that night. Yep, the price might be pretty big, but heck, it would be worth it! No one should waste such a fine day! The outdoors and the beautiful world were calling to him—all his to enjoy. Shoot! Being out here instead of sitting all day in that chair doing schoolwork.... Of course, it's worth it!

As he skipped along the trail beneath familiar boughs he saw a red bird chirping in a tree. "Howdy Mr. Redbird," he yelled gleefully. Below him, the river flowed smoothly between high cliffs of rich farm soil. Approaching a small bend where the river turned beneath the cliffs, he spied one particular oak tree standing right on the edge and marveled at the extent of the roots spidering down through the soil toward the river. "This is the spot!" he said out loud. He sat down, reached into his right overall pocket and pulled out a small spool of black thread. Two days earlier, when his mother sat working at her sewing table, Bobby had asked if he might have some thread. When she asked why, he had explained, "I'm going to use it the next time I go fishing." Unable to resist his boyish grin and bright blue eyes, she had handed over a nearly full spool of thread. He now unwound it a few inches then dug into his other pocket to retrieve the hook he had set into an orange peel saved from breakfast that morning.

Working skillfully, he fastened the hook to the thread with a knot of his own creation, three turns to the right, through the eye again and back through the loop. No fish in the world would ever be able to break the line off this hook! Once satisfied, he carefully stuck the hook, with line attached, into the bark of a nearby cottonwood tree.

Bobby stood, stretched his arms to heaven in absolute bliss and then looked down the path for another special tree. He scanned the trees along the river bank for just the right one to provide a suitable pole for the day. There it was, just like last time… a branch in the big Castor Bean tree. The branches jutted out graciously toward the water and almost seemed to beckon him. Last time around this particular tree had provided a really great fishing pole but that one became lost when he had hidden it on the bank before heading home. Turns out, a real gully-washer of a rain had washed his prize piece of angling equipment down the Colorado toward well, who knows where?

The branch he spotted was about eight feet or so up so Bobby launched himself into the tree and, climbing as best he could, got a good hold of the branch near its joint with the trunk. With his other hand he grabbed further along the branch and pushed off the trunk with his feet. Snap! Down he fell, branch in hand. His new pole was about six feet long. Yippee! He laughed again and began removing smaller green branches from his new fishing pole.

From his pocket he took out his prized folding Scout pocketknife that his daddy had given him and now smoothed the branch's joints. Perfect. Bobby stood and returned up the trail to his cottonwood tree, retrieved the spool of line and his hook, and sat down on the bank to assemble his fishing pole. Just at that spot, the flowing water had carved an incredibly deep water hole where fish would lie in wait for drifting delicacies heading toward the Gulf of Mexico.

And in that pool was a big fat black bass. This he knew for sure. He knew because he had missed him last time out. He had gotten too excited when the fish had taken his grasshopper-worm combination bait, and he had yanked the line in too quickly before the fish had swallowed the hook. Well, live and learn like daddy said! On that day, he vowed he would return and catch that rascal bass for sure next time. "Well, fish, the next time is here so get ready!"

Bobby Meyer then gleefully tossed a new, even-more-enticing, grasshopper-worm-frog combination bait into the quiet waters of the Colorado River that morning literally vibrating with excitement about the fishing action he knew was coming.

BUILDING YOUNG MEN: GOD'S GIFTS

Romans 12:6. "We have different gifts, according to the grace given us."

Times have certainly changed since that day in 1942. While this is a colossal understatement of social and cultural fact, the truth is, boys still crave and seek adventure. Boys are still boys. The reality is that they are hardwired to seek out adventure and will pursue it no matter what the cost, to themselves or others. Bobby Meyer's interests in the outdoors were apparent even as a very young boy. When he grew into a man, Bob created Meyer's Mountain Men of Austin, Texas. This camp became famous as one of the most effective outreach tools for boys ever conceived, offering extended travel-camping adventures throughout the American West.

Later in life, Bob explained it was "the beauty of God's handiwork in nature" that presented him such an exciting lure his entire life. He always enjoyed and found renewal in spending time outdoors camping, hiking and fishing. And for forty-four years, from 1958 to 1996, Bob traveled the west from Texas to Alaska with over 3,000 young men and shared his knowledge of the outdoors. This type of experience was then, and is still today, a vital ingredient needed by young men to help them along the path of learning about themselves in order to become strong and capable adult men.

We are all born with gifts. Some call these our innate abilities. Some people ascribe personality traits exclusively to genetics. Others say personality results from environmental development. Still others say it is a combination of both. Whatever you believe, everyone has a distinct personality no matter how it arrives or develops. If you take time, looking really closely, you will find that everyone leans toward certain interests in life. These tendencies or interests are based upon the inherent gifts, strengths or abilities. And throughout time young men have always struggled to identify these strengths and how to use them on their road to manhood. Today in our hyper-connected and yet socially fractured world, all too often others tend to point out a boy's strengths to him as weaknesses, especially during adolescence. As he strives to find his place in the world, his self-image often becomes defined by the culture around him. Dependent upon the culture this can be a very good thing, but sometimes it can produce very bad results. His inherent God-given gifts—those all-important abilities and interests forming his core personality—may be brushed aside even unintentionally for what is considered to be in his best interests.

The Bob Meyer vignette shows a young man whose personality demonstrated strong will, energy, creativity, determination and passion for the outdoors over the indoor world. Given a choice, Bob would rather be outside any day rather than inside—a life-shaping observation, simple but powerful. For even against the advice of his daddy, Bob followed his dreams. His gift of teaching and his love of people and of the outdoors evolved into providing camping and learning opportunities that were unique and life-changing for countless young men as they explored and adventured their way throughout the American West.

Consider the Boys in Your Life....

The importance of taking time to learn to identify a young man's inherent strengths and then teaching him how to use them in different situations cannot be over emphasized. What new interests have you seen appear? What abilities have you noticed and what new skills are your boys working on trying to improve? Have you looked lately? Here is a challenge: can you accurately recognize and describe your child right now in ten words or less? Take time to investigate by spending undivided time with your youngsters. Arrange something new to do together outside. There is nothing like a hike, a bike ride or just a simple walk together. Or, like Bob Meyer, go fishing. Leave the electronics behind so you can be in the moment together. You will both be amazed at the results.

THE SKY-VUE

La Mesa, Texas, July, 2005

"Honesty is the first chapter of the book of wisdom."
—Thomas Jefferson

I t was a late July afternoon as the bus carrying the Mountain Men rolled slowly through the sparsely populated streets of LaMesa. We were heading south enroute to a landmark icon in West Texas, the Sky-Vue Drive-in theatre. Named after the Spanish term "table-land," LaMesa is a community located between Lubbock, Midland and Abilene. For most of the world, this location may best be understood as just to the west and north of the middle of nowhere.

The Mountain Men were returning home after a twenty-five day leadership-adventure camp throughout the western United States and Canada. In reaching LaMesa, we were still a day-and-a-half away from our home base in Georgetown, Texas. LaMesa offered a key stop for entertainment in the last days of camp. Sam and Carolyn Kirkland, the gracious owners of the Sky-Vue and friends of the

Mountain Men, were looking forward to the boys coming to watch a double feature on the big screen. As the bus headed south out of town down Highway 87, the boys spied the famous sign on the left. The marquee was lit up with colored lights showing the night's features, *Herbie* and *Madagascar.*

The volume of voices rose incredibly as the bus pulled in. Inside the ticket booth the high-school-age employee recognized the white camp bus with the elk antlers mounted on top, and with a smile he waved us through. We parked parallel to the big screen at the back of the lot. I opened the door, and immediately twenty-five young men piled out of the bus and ran directly to the snack bar. Already people had set up lawn chairs or were using pick-up truck tailgates for movie-viewing. Laughter and a palpable lightness of spirit were flowing through the air. The temperature was warm but not unpleasant, and a very light breeze gently touched the hundreds of patrons settling in during the rapidly dimming light of the West Texas sky. Anticipation, camaraderie and fellowship were in full bloom at Sky-Vue this summer evening.

Two campers, Jimmy and Tyler, were already in line at the snack bar as I sought out Sam to say hello after another year of absence. "Hey guys, what are you getting?" I asked coming through the door and heading toward the projection room, where Sam would most likely be hanging out. The boys smiled huge, teenage smiles, and Tyler said, "I'm going to get a Chihuahua, two burgers, fries and a coke to start."

"I'm going for two cheeseburgers, a hot dog and a coke," said Jimmy.

Happy people packed the snack bar. Its walls were filled with memorabilia, mostly dating back to the late '40s when the theatre first opened. It turns out that singer-songwriter Buddy Holly of the famous *Crickets* held his first gig on top of this very snack bar. No kidding. Out in front of the snack bar children were riding a metal merry-go round and swinging in swings as music was playing through speakers. A true, laid-back, small-town Americana experience, the Sky-Vue is a family entertainment destination for the people of West Texas. They prize what Sam and Carolyn have created and maintain; a place to come to with a culture of relaxed entertainment that is family oriented. This combination of hometown hospitality and relaxed entertainment brings folks in from all over, time and time again.

As I caught up with Sam, the Mountain Men spread themselves out in front of the bus, eating and drinking and watching the movies. As the last clips of *Madagascar* credits rolled, people began heading home. Tonight, the Mountain Men would call the Sky-Vue their home. The camp would stay overnight and then leave early in the morning after cleaning up the entire lot—our service thank-you to Sam and Carolyn for the camping opportunity. As the evening began to wind down it was then that Michael came up to me.

"Hey, Mikey, what's up?" I asked cheerfully.

"Hi Captain, I found this lying on the ground and thought you would know what to do with it," said Michael. He then handed me a black wallet.

"I'll see if I can figure out who this belongs to," I said. "I appreciate your bringing it to my attention." I then headed back to the snack bar, and with the key Sam had given me I opened the door. In the light I counted out $270 in cash. I wrote Sam a note explaining that Michael had found the wallet with the money inside, and that it was now safely in his desk drawer. I closed the note with another thanks for the evening and then sat down… and thought. A teenage boy had just found a wallet with over two hundred dollars in cash. He had turned it in without much ado. Awesome, I thought, awesome.

At the crack of dawn the next day, the Mountain Men were up cleaning the bus and the Sky-Vue parking lot, after which we headed home. Late that afternoon, around 4:00 p.m., Sam called. He had located the wallet's owner using some identification inside. The owner of the wallet explained to Sam that he was a college student in Canyon, Texas and had come to the movies that Friday night and lost his wallet. When Sam asked about the amount of money he was carrying, he said to the best of his knowledge he had $270. The elated owner couldn't believe the wallet and his money had been turned in. Sam then asked me if he could call Michael's parents in order to get their permission to have the story put in the LaMesa newspaper. The story of the event along with the note I wrote to Sam hangs on the wall in the Sky-Vue snack bar to this day.

At the Mountain Men's closing campfire on our last evening Michael was recognized by the staff and the camp as our outstanding camper. This was our way of honoring Michael and of showing the other young men the importance and value of the character traits of honesty and integrity.

BUILDING YOUNG MEN: HONESTY

2 Corinthians 8:21. "For we are taking pains to do what is right, not only in the eyes of the Lord but also in the eyes of men."

We should consider that if we listen to the media alone, our world seems to be sadly lacking in honesty and integrity. It seems a big, negative cauldron of "bubble, bubble, toil and trouble." Sure, there is trouble in the world, always has been and until a future unknown date, there always will be. It is interesting to note that in America good news doesn't really sell. If you are unsure, just read a newspaper. This doesn't mean good stuff isn't happening every day; it is. I firmly believe the majority of youth in America have a character reflecting honesty and integrity. They intend to be good people and are looking to do good stuff. Michael showed the camp, the community of LaMesa, Texas, his parents and friends, that doing the right thing is the right thing to do. Simple, yet profound.

Consider the Boys in Your Life....

How do your boys view truth, integrity and honesty in today's world embracing situational ethics? How do you model these character traits? And how might you introduce or reinforce the importance of these values to help them become successful men? Here's a suggestion: talk to each other. Set up some what-if scenarios and play them out to include choices and consequences. Let each boy know you value his honesty. Your goal is to build understanding and a bridge of trust so he can always come to you for advice and direction when moral dilemmas come up in his life... and they will. Will you be ready? Will he?

Here is a poem that speaks to planning to be whom we wish to be without any regrets.

Myself
Edgar A. Guest

I have to live with myself and so
I want to be fit for myself to know.
I want to be able as days go by,
always to look myself straight in the eye;
I don't want to stand with the setting sun
and hate myself for the things I have done.
I don't want to keep on a closet shelf
a lot of secrets about myself
and fool myself as I come and go
into thinking no one else will ever know
the kind of person I really am,
I don't want to dress up myself in sham.
I want to go out with my head erect
I want to deserve all men's respect;
but here in the struggle for fame and wealth
I want to be able to like myself.
I don't want to look at myself and know that
I am bluster and bluff and empty show.
I never can hide myself from me;
I see what others may never see;
I know what others may never know,
I never can fool myself and so,
whatever happens I want to be
self-respecting and conscience free.

TALKING TREES

Redwood Forest, California, 2004

*"Forests are the lungs of our land, purifying the air
and giving fresh strength to our people."*
—Theodore Roosevelt

On this June day, the Mountain Men headed into the coastal redwood forest north of San Francisco, California. With trees reaching upwards of 300 feet in some cases, the environment is nothing less than magical. All of one's senses—sight, hearing, smell, touch and even taste—are magnified in any forest setting, but among the giant redwoods, one's sensory perspectives are shifted beyond anything even remotely familiar. The spectacular dimensions of the trees cast a sense of awe on us seemingly dwarfed humans. Huge and magnificent trunks reach majestically up into the sky, their canopies swaying gently in the misty breeze. Birds dart amongst the highest branches calling out to one another. An aromatic scent of redwood offers a unique and fresh smell. Insects buzz loudly denoting an ever-moving life presence. And the forest floor, padded with the remnants of thousands of years of cyclical deposits of forest detritus, make a wonderfully spongy and comfortable foundation on which to walk.

What an incredible place to camp and explore! We found a suitable camp site and set up, and I then asked staffer Nicholas Cowey to take the twenty-six young men for a hike into the forest. My plan was to stay back and prepare the eight pounds of fresh Pacific salmon we had just purchased right off a dock on our way to the redwoods. I explained what I wanted him to do. "Discuss the natural history of the ecosystem," I said, "and take the guys away from the trails."

Nicholas is gifted with an incredible knowledge of all things natural, a photographic memory and a great sense of humor. He can entertain endlessly, especially in an environment like the redwood forest. "Somewhere along the way," I added, "I want the boys to all stay silent for fifteen minutes minimum. You know, no talking, no laughing, no giggling, no horseplay, just silent while they look up into those magnificent trees and around at the forest."

"Got it," Nicholas said quickly. He called the campers together, and they headed off around a corner and disappeared into the Redwoods.

Meanwhile, I began preparing a meal of grilled salmon, roasted potatoes and a fresh green salad. I also stirred up our dessert specialty, Mountain Men Cobblers. This evening I planned two; one blackberry-blueberry and the other, peach. As time progressed, the salmon and vegetables were cooking nicely, smells of butter, garlic and salmon mixing with the aroma of redwoods. The cobblers were also underway, and I now had the place virtually to myself. I did have company from Grady, our Golden Retriever camp dog. As an official member of the Mountain Men staff, he has traveled with us through every western state, two provinces of Canada and Alaska. Grady lay relaxed and quiet at my feet while I sat down to write in my journal for a few minutes.

With clear skies and the temperature around 52 degrees, the redwood forest was really peaceful. Wow, was it ever quiet. Not a sound except for the occasional passing call of a Stellar Jay hoping for a freebie from the camp kitchen. I sat transfixed by the moment, all my senses tuned to the smells, temperature, quiet and majesty of one of God's most marvelous creations, the redwoods.

These trees are the largest living thing on Earth and some of the oldest as well. Scientists have documented some specimens being over 3,000 years old. This unique ecosystem stretches along the Pacific coast from central California to southern Oregon. Once, back in the 1850s, the forests covered an area of over two million acres. Today 95 percent of the original, old growth forests are gone, down to just a few hundreds of thousands of acres, as a result of massive clear cutting during the Gold Rush and post-World War II expansion eras. This magnificent ecosystem is the only one like it on our planet. Fortunately, forward-thinking conservationists took action and helped influence state and federal officials to begin setting aside some of these remarkable resources for future generations to enjoy. Today, there are a significant number of state and national parks throughout California where people can experience the majesty and beauty of these old growth redwoods.

Lost in thought, I recorded the day's event in my journal. I made some notes about the boys personalities, the group dynamics and our many activities—the reflective process being a source of satisfaction. I felt deeply thankful for the opportunity to lead young men as they discovered the beauty of God's handiwork in nature here in such a magnificent place.

I was brought back to reality as the boys returned, hungry and anxious to tell about their experiences. I listened quietly to several stories and then suggested we might save the rest for our campfire. That way everyone could hear every story. Surprisingly, all agreed.

After dinner as the fire was burning down and the cobbler had vanished, we assembled around the campfire. Usually we start off with some sort of story about the area, based loosely on a local or historical character and then twisted into an adventurous tall tale that might include ghosts, creatures of the dark or other scary elements. Tonight, however, seemed different. Everyone was more relaxed than usual. It wasn't due to the large amount of food, as our Mountain Men always have large meals. No, something different had their attention.

As we stared into the fire, I asked Nicholas to offer a reflection on the day's activities. He was dressed in an 1803 era caped hunting frock identical to what Lewis and Clark wore during their famous expedition out west. On his head was a raccoon fur hat, a real one, hand stitched by himself. Lit by flickers of the fire light, he brought to life a story about the Native Americans living back in times before white men had arrived. As his story progressed, he went into the natural history of the redwood ecosystem and what the boys had explored this day.

The young, modern-day Mountain Men sat transfixed, listening to every word while watching the fire wave and dance about. It was a magical moment. Here were boys at their most impressionable best, their imaginations and senses fully opened, when everything felt possible. "Who would like to be first to share what's he's learned on today's hike so everyone can benefit?" asked Nicholas. "We'll go in order around the circle."

When it became their turn boy after boy told of experiencing incredible beauty and a sense of quiet and peacefulness in the forest. They talked of birds and ferns, animal tracks in the detritus and the soft padded ground to walk on. Of course, their recollections included the amazing trees, their tops generally enshrouded in mist, the notice of occasional touches of blue sky peeking through. They recounted new smells that were fresh and unusual, especially the redwood. There were stories of sightings of high-flying osprey and inquisitive squirrels. About halfway around the circle it became the turn of yet another young Mountain Man. When asked about his impressions, he said, "I didn't know that trees could talk."

I looked across the fire into the gently lit face and asked, "What did the trees say to you?" Without skipping a beat, he continued, "They said they were very, very old. They said they remember when the Indians lived here and moved quietly along the forest floor. They even remembered when there were no Indians, just birds and animals living in the forest."

"How do they speak?" I inquired.

"They creak and groan their words as they sway in the breeze high up. They are really tall, you know, so they are up there in the sky where the wind lives. They can see forever."

I was thrilled with the imagination, or was it imagination? From here the circle of reflection continued to become more introspective. The next young man explained that as he gazed up hundreds of feet into the upper branches of the trees he had felt peaceful, quiet and thankful for his life. He said, "They are really alive protecting those down below like us."

Story after story began to unfold with similar content: all about peace, quiet, tranquility, protection, magnificence and reverence. We ended our fire quietly that evening giving thanks once more, this time collectively, for the opportunities we had enjoyed that day. No ghost stories were shared nor requested. No adrenaline-producing, fear-evoking tales of imagination that boys most often like to hear around a fire. Not tonight. Tonight had been a most unusual first-person moment when boys shared their individual encounters with peace, solitude and introspection.

For some, this day and evening may have been the first time they actually experienced real peace and quiet. Hopefully, this adventure will be long-remembered, a memory the Mountain Men can return to that will help quiet and soothe their minds later on when the busyness and noise of life presses in on them.

BUILDING YOUNG MEN: PEACE, SOLITUDE AND INTROSPECTION

Psalm 46:10. "Be still and know that I am God."

Throughout time men have sought and continue to seek peace. Peace and quiet. This state of mind is often hard to find in today's busy world. Webster's Dictionary offers this suggestion of what peace is: "a state of quiet or tranquility; freedom from disturbance or agitation; calm, repose." Sounds great doesn't it? Wouldn't that be nice sometimes?

Indeed, how often do you feel stressed from over-communication or over-activity? If you do, you are not alone. Our cell phones go everywhere with us, always on so we do not miss that next important call, text or email, or a YouTube, Twitter, Facebook, Instagram, Skype or LinkedIn connection. Using that little device, we work, communicate and play online. While entertaining and perhaps helpful in keeping up, this hyper-connectedness is sadly sometimes producing new and unexpected maladies for mental and physical health. In her recent book, *The Big Disconnect: Protecting Childhood and Family Relationships in the Digital Age,* Catherine Steiner-Adair, a researcher and clinical instructor of Psychiatry at Harvard, shows how too much of any variety of "screen use" can compromise relationships and impede normal social and emotional development in children.

Think with me for a moment: if you often feel stressed and restless, imagine what it must be like for our children. According to *Nielsen,* a global information measurement company, kids between the ages of twelve and seventeen send an estimated 3,400 texts per month or, on average, seven texts per hour. Wow. How do you think this may affect their peace of mind? Parents have to decide for themselves and their children how much connectedness is ideal and healthy. What are the tradeoffs between convenience, connectedness and peace and quiet? We need to think about that and understand what is actually going on.

What is certain is that all men need peace, quiet and time to think. Sometimes regular guys try sports or hobbies to find peace. But I'm suggesting something still deeper, something in nature. World leaders escape daily pressures through these types of retreats. Jesus himself regularly retired to the mountains seeking introspection and private prayer time and communion with the Father. We are still the same men today.

Maybe it's time we stop adjusting without question to the latest technological change. Boys need an extended amount of time to sort through all the myriad stimuli coming at them. They need time to develop the skills and abilities to discern right from wrong, to make good decisions and to learn patience. That evening among the redwoods—when the boys brought up the "talking trees"—shows how deeply they crave peace, solitude and introspection.

Consider the Boys in Your Life....

Do you or your boys have any boundaries on the use of technology? Do you have times designated that are off-limits for technology, to assure family communications? What would it look like if you were playing board games with your boys or they were reading or playing outside instead of being consumed by the world of electronics? What might happen? Do something different today. Here's an idea: take your kids outside. Lie down on a blanket and look up at the sky, smell the smells of your world, close your eyes, listen to the sounds you hear. As you relax, think of everything you are thankful for. Ask your kids to think the same then share your experiences over dinner. Try to help them recount everything they saw, smelled and heard and what they are thankful for. The goal is for you to create an environment where peace of mind can be achieved. Leave the electronics behind. You'll be surprised what will happen!

Chapter 4 — Good and Evil

The Truth of the Matter

Stillwell Ranch, Texas, March 2007

"The first idea the child must acquire is that of the difference between good and evil."

—Maria Montessori

This spring day found us hiking and exploring the vastness of Big Bend National Park, in far West Texas. Added in 1944 as the twenty-seventh treasure in our country's system of national parks, Big Bend is amazing. As the eighth largest park it covers some 801,000 acres and offers a virtual smorgasbord of geology, flora and fauna, with many unique features. From the northern Chihuahua desert basins into the Chisos Mountains and on to the famous Rio Grande Wild & Scenic River bordering Mexico, this park has an aura of significance. Throughout the day, the twenty-five young Mountain Men explored the mysteries of Dog Canyon and later tumbled down the sand dunes of Boquillas Canyon. They soaked in the hot springs on the edge of the Rio Grande just enjoying being boys in the outdoors with no other responsibilities or requirements other than to have fun. These new experiences brought carefree laughter and joy into every boy's heart.

Later, as we settled down into camp that night, coyotes occasionally yelped out their sad calls interrupting the silence to let us know we had invaded their territory. After a restful outdoor sleep, morning broke upon us across the desert with a clear blue sky, the sun rising smartly across the creosote bushes with hawks already circling lazily above. Breakfast today was a special treat, Hole in the Walls with all the fixings! That meant large pieces of Texas Toast with the centers torn out, buttered on both sides and then tossed onto a hot grill with an egg placed in the middle. There is nothing like a Mountain Man breakfast! What a great start to a day of adventure!

Soon it was time for our leadership lesson. After cleaning up our "kitchen" and the inside of our travel bus, our Mountain Men lined up alongside the bus. "Guys," I said, "today we are going to talk about good and evil. I want you to think about the most evil thing you can imagine. I am not going to ask you to talk about it or discuss it with anyone. I just want you to think about it."

Everyone became quiet. After a moment, I asked the first young man in the line to tell me what he thought evil was.

"Evil is when you do something really bad that you know you shouldn't have done," he said.

"Good thought, I replied moving to the next boy. "What do you think evil is?"

"I think evil is when bad things happen to people and they didn't deserve it."

I acknowledged that idea and kept moving to the next boy. One young man said, "I think evil is an opinion," which made me pause.

47

With all inquiries completed, I turned to two staff members holding a duffel bag and asked them to show what was inside. They reached inside and pulled out a flag for all to see. Lit from behind by the sun, the flag was bright red with a large swastika sitting in a white circle. I expected the boys to ooh and ahh but instead I received a stunned silence. I asked, "Do you know what this is?"

One boy immediately exclaimed, "That's a Nazi flag!"

"That's right," I said. "This is a real Nazi flag." I then told them its history, with the twisted ideals of Hitler's use of the symbolism of the flag to show the nature of the nationalistic, social movement and the struggle for the so-called Aryan man. I explained that it was under the influence of this flag that the world was plunged into world war and millions of innocent men, women and children were slaughtered. I then told the staff to put away the flag. They stuffed it back into the duffel bag, which they threw on the ground. Then a staff guy brought me a second duffel. I reached into it and pulled out another object. "Boys, do you know what this is?" I asked as a familiar shape and color emerged from the bag. The boys nodded.

"That's an American flag!" several shouted out in unison.

"Right again!" I said. "How do you know it is an American flag?"

"Because of the stars and colors," said one boy.

"Sure, but why is it folded in tricorn?" I asked. "Why is it red, white and blue? And how many folds are in this flag?" Sadly, no one knew. I then explained the reason for the colors: red for the blood, bravery and valor that led to our freedom; white for honesty, truth and piety within our country; and blue for the sky, heavens and God. The stars for our fifty states. I told them the reasons for the thirteen folds: thirteen for the thirteen original colonies.

I also related how each fold, although unofficial, carries for many a special significance. Fold number one, a symbol of life. Two, for our belief in eternal life. Three, for remembrance of our veterans who fought and died that we may remain free. Four, for our trust in God and his divine guidance. The fifth, a tribute to our country. The sixth, for where our hearts lie, in allegiance to our flag, our country, the Republic for which it stands, One Nation, under God, indivisible, with Liberty and Justice for all. The seventh fold, in tribute to our Armed Forces that protect our country against all enemies. The eighth, in tribute to the one who entered the valley of the shadow of death, that we might see the light of day. The ninth, in tribute to mothers whose faith, love, loyalty and devotion have molded the character of this nation. The tenth, in tribute to the fathers who have given their sons and daughters for defense of this country. The eleventh, a symbol of David and Solomon, in glory to the God of Abraham and Isaac. The twelfth, an emblem of eternity, and in the Christians' eyes, a symbol of God the Father, The Son and the Holy Spirit.

"The final fold, the thirteenth fold," I said, "with the stars uppermost, reminds us of our nation's motto, In God We Trust." Finally, knowing that the tricorn shape of our flag represents different things to different people I asked the boys, "Why do you think our flag is folded in tricorn and not square or rectangular?"

This generated lots of ideas. One boy suggested, "Is it folded in tricorn because a triangle is the strongest shape in geometry and our country is the strongest country in the world?" Another boy said, "The flag is folded in tricorn because each point represents the three branches of our government, the legislative, judicial and executive branches." Another of our group thought it was representative of the

49

triune God; the Father, the Son and the Holy Spirit because most of the founding fathers were Christian believers.

"Although truly unknown as to when the folding etiquette began or why," I said, "most people today believe that the triangular fold is in honor of the tricorn shape of the hats worn by soldiers who fought for independence under General George Washington. But all your ideas have relevance and credibility." At this point one boy exclaimed, "I didn't know this stuff! Why don't they teach us this in school?" I simply responded, "Good question. Primarily because public schools fear violation of someone's civil rights and don't wish to be sued so avoid discussions of religious beliefs." And with that I moved the discussion back to the two flags.

"Guys, let me tell you the history of these flags," I said. "Both flags belong to the family of Major James Robert Brown, my father-in-law, now deceased. Major Brown was an officer in the 42nd Infantry Rainbow Division of the U.S. Army, a group of military men who liberated a Nazi concentration camp called Dachau. And that is where this Nazi flag is believed to have been flown." I pointed to the crumpled duffel bag on the ground containing the Nazi flag. "That Nazi flag represents a time in history when a group of people believed that slaughtering millions of innocent men, women and children was okay. That was a time when the entire world was engulfed in war. The American flag shown to you today has not been unfurled nor seen the light of day since it draped the casket of Major Brown at his funeral. That American flag represents the men and women like Major Brown who fought to free the people being oppressed under that other flag. These soldiers knew firsthand that both good and evil do exist. They were men and women willing to fight and to die to protect the freedoms you and I enjoy today."

"Evil does in fact still exist today," I continued. "It is not an opinion but is very, very real. Just because no one is shooting at us we may think that we are insulated from evil in our modern American life but I can tell you, we are not. Evil will come before each of us. It comes in many forms besides war. We will be tried and challenged, often at our weakest point. For some of us it may challenge our honesty, for others our courage, for others our integrity. Whatever our weakness as a man, it will attack us. The good news is this: we can resist evil and overcome it! Thank God we live in a free society where we can make good choices. So let's learn from the past and become true men of character. We can all do it!"

BUILDING YOUNG MEN: GOOD AND EVIL

Proverbs 22:6. "Train a child in the way he should go,
and when he is old he will not turn from it."

Look on the front page of virtually any newspaper in the country and you'll see that evil exists. In America, moral lawlessness, evil and sin are often sadly viewed as a situational occurrence, an opinion versus a reality, as one young man expressed at the camp. Today the stand for political correctness and determination for the right to say or do anything, no matter what the consequences imposed on others, is of paramount importance to those demanding total equality of rights. Contrast that to World War II when it was very clear what was good and what was evil.

Today we often seem to have real difficulty in making clear distinctions between good and evil. Why? If you study history you will find that Germany fell prey to Hitler's evil much the same way you boil a frog. Put the frog in warm, not hot water, and slowly turn up the heat until he boils to death. By the time the people of Germany realized what was really happening they had become powerless to stop the Nazi movement. In like fashion, our society has slowly been turning up the heat on what is considered acceptable practices until you can look around today and find the most bizarre, deviant behaviors—and yet, such behaviors are expected to be accepted and protected as rights. As culture evolves, keep in mind that good is also here and openly available for all of us as a choice.

Consider the Boys in Your Life....

Do your boys know the difference between good and evil? Are they able to distinguish between the two in today's clouded world of mixed values and technology? As parents, it is our duty to protect those who are weaker than ourselves, to provide guidance and support along their paths to adulthood. So do your young men understand choices and consequences? Be aware of reality, take a stand and set boundaries. An odd reality is that children crave boundaries, which give them security. Sometimes today parents get this confused. In their zeal to be close to their kids they choose to set up friendships instead of setting boundaries. This does not produce successful character in adulthood. So choose to have a discussion; describe examples of good and evil, and ask their opinions. Then by your own example lead them along the paths of goodness. Set boundaries and do not be fearful of pushback from your kids. Show them the way to a peaceful, enjoyable and successful life based on dependence on Christ; they will love you for it!

DIVINE APPOINTMENTS

Johnstown, Colorado, June 2012

"Purpose within yourself to stop missing divine appointments."

—Galena R. Conaster, *Running to Win*

L ife at 55 mph seems slow to most of us in our high-speed, instant-on, always-connected world. However, in a bus with twenty-five other people, most under the age of sixteen, it is just about right. There is actually time to see what is passing by and time to play, talk and laugh. Such was the day for the Mountain Men on a late summer afternoon tooling along I-25 north of Denver, headed for Cheyenne, Wyoming. I was driving the bus when suddenly a mechanical racket began beneath me, shuddered up through the shifter and caused a loss of power.

Immediately, I put the now-useless transmission into neutral and checked the mirrors to see what the traffic looked like on the right. One quarter mile or so ahead, there was an exit ramp. Another quarter mile up that road was a major truck stop. "Can you spot anyone driving down the access road on the right?" I asked my staff. "If not, I am not slowing down for the upcoming exit." No traffic coming, they said. Nothing entering or exiting the truck stop either. I put on my blinker and turned onto the access road. Using the momentum of the 26,000-pound vehicle traveling at almost 55 mph we began to coast toward the truck stop. With no traffic, we rolled in, zooming past huge, parked semi-trailers, and then pulled into an open spot between two semis at the end of the parking area.

With an anxious sigh, I turned off the ignition. I told one of my staff to go check the area for safety, then to get the campers off the bus and let them stretch their legs. My son Ryan, who was driving the chuck wagon with all the food, pulled up and asked what was happening. After filling him in on our dilemma, we crawled under the bus in hopes of seeing something that would clue us in to what had caused the loss of power. Nothing was evident, but then again, we aren't mechanics.

We are scientists and school teachers. Here I was a camp director and teacher taking kids on a three-week adventure to Yellowstone National Park and our mode of transportation was now broken. Time schedules, cost factors, entertainment concerns and reputation of the camp all at risk within just one second of change. One minute, happily headed for Yellowstone, the next minute parked in an unknown truck stop with no ability to drive the machine and zero understanding of what was wrong.

A trucker came over. We pulled the cowling away from the engine so he could look around. He asked a few questions. "Sorry," he said after a few minutes. "I don't know what's wrong. A truck repair shop is over there on the right. Maybe they can help."

After thanking him I went looking for the repair shop. Sure enough up on the right, I spotted it just past a little church for truckers. Three guys in the shop were putting stuff together around a rig. I explained we were from a camp and that our bus had broken down. "Could you help us out?" I inquired. "No, sorry," was the answer. "We've closed, and this shop is in the process of moving. Our tools and spare parts are already at the new shop twenty miles down the road. Maybe you can call another place."

We called two truck repair shops and left messages. Now that it was coming close to six o'clock, most places appeared to be closed for the day. As we were walking back to the bus, passing the truckers' church, I noticed a Texas A&M sticker on the back window of a car parked on the side of the building. I am an Aggie graduate, so taking the initiative, I went to the front of the building. A sign on the door said, "All Are Welcome." I went in, and a man inside greeted me. Turns out, his name is Bill Reily, and Chaplain Bill is also an Aggie, an Eagle Scout and is now a minister to thousands of people who drive trucks up and down I-25. We talked awhile and I explained my situation.

"The boys can sleep behind the church building," Bill said unhesitatingly. "They can use the facilities for restrooms and grab water, etc., whatever is needed."

Wow. A safe haven from the world, quite literally in God's backyard. The boys thought this all quite exciting. Meanwhile, I was still anxiously trying to figure out how to entertain the youngsters and save the camp from economic disaster. I had my son find out the cost to rent two fifteen passenger vans for two weeks. Suffice it to say, we were in a serious bind.

I went for a walk by myself to think and pray. It came to me to call my mechanic friend back in Texas. I went back to the bus and dialed up Dennis Fidler who had been taking care of this particular bus for the last ten years. Dennis is a remarkable mechanic, a real friend and a man of God. I caught him at dinner with his wife. "Hey Ron! Where are you guys?" he asked.

"We are outside of Loveland, Colorado," I said. "The bus is broken. I need your advice. Do you have a minute?" I went on to explain the noises, the failure of propulsion and suggested maybe I had somehow torn the transmission to smithereens.

Dennis was not so sure. He had me explain again what was going on so I recited everything in order to the best of my ability. He then had me turn on the ignition and hold the cell phone down near the engine and above the shifter. There was a silence. "Go outside," he said. "Chock the wheels, put the transmission into neutral, lock the parking brake and put the cell phone up next to the differential housing. I want to listen."

Dennis went on, describing the housing, shape, numbers, etc. that he wanted us to look for. So, at his direction, Ryan and I climbed under the bus and crawled to the differential housing and found the part that Dennis had described. We held the cell phone up next to the housing, the clattering noise clearly obvious to Dennis. We climbed back out from under the bus and talked with Dennis. He said, "Ron, what I think you have is a two-speed linear actuator failure." I responded, "A what?" I did not understand a thing he had just said. Dennis went on, "The differential housing has a board with a computer chip in it that controls the high and low gears within the differential," he explained. "If it fails, the gears don't know which level to be in so they cycle continuously and never engage high or low. The result is a loss of power because the transmission will not engage so there is no pulling-power to the wheels. Actually, it's a pretty easy fix if you can find a part but that might be difficult."

By now it was 8:30 p.m. No stores were open, and with our kids needing attention, we fed the campers and settled in for the night.

Next morning early, Ryan got on the phone and called all the automotive distribution parts places in Denver and surrounding areas. He finally found the needed part in north Denver, approximately thirty-five miles away. "I'm going to get the part," I told my number two staffer. "While I'm gone I want Mr. Reily's place cleaned, mowed and polished up in appreciation for allowing us to camp here."

Ryan and I took off in the chuck wagon, found the place for truck parts and bought our part. Within forty-five minutes Ryan installed the new part; we tested everything and were back in business! The boys had done a marvelous job of cleaning up Chaplain Bill's church and the grounds around it. I stopped in once more to talk to Bill. "Before we leave," I asked him, "can you say a few words of encouragement to the boys?"

We circled up behind the church and Chaplain Bill shared some thoughts. "Your coming here was not an accident," he said. "We were all supposed to meet here to have this discussion." He talked about manhood, the importance of scouting and learning in life not to panic when things happen and then closed by asking God's blessings on the boys and on the camp. As a servant of God, Bill gives of himself to help others down the road, literally and figuratively, every single day of the year. Today, through God's direction, he helped inspire all of us.

I thanked Bill again. We climbed happily aboard the bus and headed for Wyoming, without another mechanical issue. Throughout the rest of the camp, the boys and staff alike discussed the meeting with Chaplain Bill at the truck stop. Was it a coincidence that our propulsion fouled exactly where we had enough momentum to exit the highway without power into a truck stop? One tenth of a mile, more or less, and we would have ended up stranded on I-25.

What about the traffic? Was it coincidental there wasn't any traffic on the access road as we coasted off I-25 and then entered one of the busiest truck stops I have ever seen, never encountering even one semi entering or departing? Was it a coincidence that we met Bill Reily right where we landed and that he runs a small church, also right there? Was it a coincidence that he is an Aggie, a member of my collegiate alma mater? What about his being an Eagle Scout, or that he was even there that day? He told me later that he is in the next town much of the time. Was it a coincidence that my mechanic was home at the exact moment I called and diagnosed the mechanical failure from sound coming over a cell phone held underneath the bus? And what about the bus part? Was it a coincidence that we called all the biggest parts stores in northern Colorado and there was only one part available in all of Denver? What about the fact that the part was located in the store closest to us? Or that when we showed up to buy the part, the clerk said it had been on the shelf a really long time, and he was amazed they even had one since they are old models and the store doesn't usually stock them. What about the fact that Ryan isn't a mechanic but was able to correctly remove and replace the part using our limited tool box in just forty-five minutes with no instructions?

Was all this a coincidence? Judge for yourself; I think not.

On many other occasions in my life, God has arranged what I have come to understand as "divine appointments." These appointments are always amazing and always offer insight when recognizing them for what they are: an opportunity to meet God face to face through people around us and to affirm faith and confidence in our Creator.

The young Mountain Men were able to experience God firsthand through such a divine appointment in Colorado, and the adventure had only just begun.

BUILDING YOUNG MEN: GOD IS IN CHARGE

Proverbs 16:9. "In his heart a man plans his course but the Lord determines his steps."

I am of the opinion that God can manifest himself around us to help us realize he is here and that he loves us. He has plans for our lives that, I believe, we can affect for good or bad by our free-will choices. And no question as men, we love to plan our ways. We go to great lengths to orchestrate our lives, our careers, our days. Our culture is achievement-oriented so there is no shortage of opportunities to get help making these plans. Even so, many of us often miss our mark. Why? I go back to the concept of alignment of our passions, skills and abilities.

The sooner we can become aware of them, the better. This will help us make decisions that will lead to a life as God intended, or if left unaligned, will add tangle and frustration to our days. So stop and reflect honestly about where you are now and how you are doing. Are you on track? Or are you headed off the tracks, toward a crash down the hillside and in need of guidance and alignment? I challenge you to go study scriptures and see what you learn about life and God's intentions for us. Try reading through Proverbs first.

As you get your own life in order you will, most wondrously, be better prepared to guide your young men similarly.

Consider the Boys in Your Life….

Think back on your life. Is there a time when you were amazed at a coincidence? A chance meeting with someone, a lucky break, a close call that went your way? Humans are skeptical creatures. We like to be in charge of all that happens to us. After all, isn't life for us and all about us? But guess what? We are not in charge. God is. Look forward as you take the next steps of your life and be sensitive to people who just sort of show up, to things that seem to happen. And then take a moment to stop and think. See what you come up with. Teach your boys how to become sensitive to other people by noticing their needs, their challenges and their gifts. This practice will help them grow socially and emotionally. Along the way, you will both start to notice divine appointments. Enjoy them as a testimony to God's presence in your lives.

ADRENALINE!

Petersburg, Alaska, June 2008

"It seems to me that the natural world is the greatest source of excitement; the greatest source of visual beauty; the greatest source of intellectual interest. It is the greatest source of so much in life that makes life worth living."

—David Attenborough

Everyone that morning was wondering, "What the heck is a jet boat anyway?" Over the last two days those conversations had evolved into a variety of interesting ideas. And today was the day they would actually find out. After a huge breakfast, our group of twenty-eight young Mountain Men walked happily down the hill from the school where we were camped about three blocks toward the docks on the Pacific Ocean. We were in the small fishing village of Petersburg, Alaska. The bay spread magnificently before us as we gazed across the Frederick Sound. The calm waters, surrounded by snow-covered mountains, were attended by busy gulls, cranes, eagles, Stellar Jays and loads of busy fishermen and their boats. The lifeblood of the community centers around the bountiful ocean, the canneries and supporting businesses.

Originating long ago as a Norwegian fishing village and now slowly coming into the 21st Century, Petersburg is real Alaska. Its people are hard-working, kind and very generous—a rare type of human. Clearly, these people understand life at its most fundamental level and appreciate it. Character, integrity, taking care of self, family and others, that's how people operate here. There isn't much room for self-centeredness or self-pity, for life can be ruthless and unforgiving to the inattentive, lazy or disinterested. With an abundance of bears prowling about, humans are not at the top of the food chain here. And for the almost 3,000 residents, the school and attached community center are the center of activities, and the Petersburg Vikings, the school system's mascot, are the pride of the village.

Indeed, everyone knows everyone. Try growing up as a boy in a situation like this. Pretty quickly, everyone knows the good and the bad. With blue-ribbon schools and a dropout rate of less than 0.5% this small town keeps people connected. Wonderfully, this village has not been marred by becoming a cruise ship destination, thus retaining a cultural identity that is full, rich and unique. So, it's no surprise: in 2013 Petersburg was named by the popular website NerdWallet.com as "The Best Town in Alaska for Young Families."

Just as we headed down the gangplank of the dock we saw a small boat speeding our way. Soon another appeared from around the bend, both seemingly on a mission. In just moments, the boats pulled up. Boys jumped up and down. These were the jet boats coming in from Wrangell. Instead of propellers like regular boats, they use impellers to compress water and push the boat forward... fast! They are much more responsive than prop-driven boats and have no downward engine shaft or propellers to be destroyed by ice, which we would soon find out was important.

Our crew split quickly into the two boats with our dog Grady joining me on the *Stikine Dream*. Within minutes the pilots had turned the vessels out toward the entrance of the harbor, revved them up and we were heading into the Inside Passage, a coastal network of inner passages weaving along the Pacific Ocean and hugging the Alaska coastline. We passed a National Geographic research ship off to our left. On our right, seals lounging on the bases of large orange buoys watched us curiously. Fanning the boys' excitement, our boats seemed to be racing each other out toward the ocean. We turned slightly north and then east into the middle of the Inside Passage. Now we're talking excitement!

"Wow, look, a whale breaching!" yelled one youngster. The adventure was all-consuming with every fiber of our being electrified and alive. We were all, as we like to say, in the moment.

A few minutes later we headed into the entrance of LeConte Bay. Soon we began to notice small pieces of ice floating past us heading out into the passage and the open ocean. The bay became narrower and the pieces of ice larger and larger. Our boats slowed and navigated between icebergs. Amazing, blue ice. Depths of color beyond description, with dazzling plays of light bouncing from within the frozen ice. Our pilots entertained us with names of icebergs associated with different sizes of ice flows such as Growlers and Bergy Bits. And then shape descriptions: Tabular, Dome, Blocky and on and on.

A completely new world was opening up before the boys' eyes. The LeConte Bay is a twelve-mile-long fjord carved out of the mountain range by glaciers over thousands of years. Eagles sat on top of bergs looking for opportunities to scavenge the area. As we continued to troll among the icebergs we passed an unusual tabular berg. Blood stains six feet or so in length looked recent. "What happened?" a boy asked soberly. Our pilot explained that local harbor seals give birth nearby and raise their pups around the bergs. Safety is an illusion, however, as predators are always lurking nearby trying to survive and continue the cycle of life. "A seal probably gave birth here," he went on, "but then a killer whale likely jumped up and took advantage of the moment."

It was a powerful life lesson for the boys. Not a staged example or a theoretical discussion but stark reality in Alaska staring them right in their young faces. The size and power of the environment, the icebergs, the chill of the water and the air all produced a sense of smallness and insignificance to our place in the world.

Finally, as we rounded a peninsula in the bay, we beheld a most incredible sight, the face of the LeConte Glacier, about a half mile away. Even at this distance, the glacier's size and magnitude were incredible! Huge, towering ice flowed directly into the ocean and ice filled the entire mountain valley behind. We were surrounded now by icebergs. Our pilots edged forward slowly, weaving methodically among the bergs, trying to get us close to the glacier's face. As we passed each berg, the boys looked down into the water and could see the gigantic foundation of the ice below.

Perspectives became skewed. Protected only by what now seemed to be minuscule aluminum boats, the boys occasionally thought about safety, as we were miles from Petersburg. They were simply stunned into silence.... What they were experiencing was real, very real. This was pure, adrenaline-producing excitement and adventure! No one knew what might come next, not even the pilots.

It was then that our pilots stopped the vessels and suggested we might wait and perhaps get lucky and see a "calving" event from the glacier ahead of us. Engines off, we drifted silently and peacefully amongst the icebergs. The only sounds were the occasional metallic bumps of ice against our boats and the sounds of boys' voices now talking excitedly. Our entire view ahead was filled with nothing but the monumental LeConte Glacier. We learned it is the largest and southernmost tide-water glacier in the northern hemisphere. It looked like a king on a throne beckoning us a bit closer. Its colors— blue, white, deep blue-white, grey, vivid and dramatic colors beyond description—filled our eyes.

Suddenly, one of the pilots got excited and pointed to the left-center of the glacier's face. "There!" he exclaimed. "Look over there."

Almost immediately a monstrous block of ice began to peel from the face. First came groaning and cracking, the ice seeming to hesitate, almost unwilling to let go and break away from the face. Then, an immense, ear-shattering crack ensued. The sound reverberated down the fjord and was immediately followed by a tremendous splashing of water. The glacier had calved! Now a hulking portion of the glacier had become yet another massive iceberg within LeConte Bay. And then we were in for a shock! Within mere seconds a huge wave generated by the berg headed right toward the boats. The iceberg had displaced water below it and with nowhere to go but out to the ocean, the wave energy zoomed down the bay toward... us.

Unnerved, excited, the boys shouted out. Our little vessels rose up several feet, then dropped back into the water with a wobbling motion. "Wow," they yelled. "That was amazing!"

Soon after, it was time for our return. Our trip back to Petersburg was one continuous adventure; a total blast—fast, fun and filled with laughter.

BUILDING YOUNG MEN: EXCITEMENT AND THRILLS

1 Timothy 4:12 "Don't let anyone look down on you because you are young, but set an example for the believers in speech, in life, in love, in faith and in purity."

Young men need to experience adventure first-hand. Movies don't replace reality, not even if viewed through 3D goggles. Video games are of no comparison. In fact, there simply is no substitute for real, true adventure. Boys crave it, need it. They seek out adventure despite pleas by mom to be careful. This is how they are hardwired. And guess what, that adventure doesn't need to be YouTubed, Tweeted, IMed, Instagrammed, texted, emailed or otherwise shared. The adventure is best enjoyed if all present are simply in the moment, not distracted with trying to capture it on video or smartphone. Just be there, fully.

Consider the Boys in Your Life....

How is the young man's hardwired need for adventure being satisfied in your world? Understandably, you don't have to arrange a jet boat ride into Alaska's LeConte Bay in order for him to experience excitement and a sense of danger. There are lots of good adventures nearby. The primary components are your time and intent commitments. Consider his age and personality as you settle on an idea.

66

Maybe canoeing, boating, gliding, flying, iFlying, zip lining, rock climbing or something else outside your and his comfort zones. Don't be scared to push it a bit. Taking along some of his friends will enhance the experience for everyone. Together, you will build shared and lasting bonds as men.

RON SMITH & BOB MEYER / NICHOLAS COWEY

LEADERSHIP & TEAM BUILDING

Fishing!

MOUNTAIN MAN BUS / HAPPY CAMPERS!

FOOD AND TARPAGE!

JET BOATS ALASKA LECONTE BAY

FRIENDS

EXPLORING NEW PLACES

FUN!

LEADERSHIP & STAFF

AWARDS NIGHT!

SEDONA & THE REDWOODS

HONOR & INTROSPECTION

RYAN LYNCH, BRIAN SMITH & DAVID PAPKE

GRADY

THE ART OF TARPAGE

Clayton Lake, New Mexico, June 2013

"You can't use up creativity. The more you use, the more you have."

—Maya Angelou

E arly on the idea of using tents fell by the wayside for the Mountain Men. While shelters are used if the threat of rain exists, the campers generally prefer to sleep on cots in the open. More than once they have awakened with snow or ice on their sleeping bags, a minor inconvenience given the experience of being out in nature. Besides tents are a hassle to put up, take down, dry out, and they never fit back into their original bags. And if a youngster is out in the open, he can see the star-filled heavens, one of the main reasons to go camping in the first place.

Over time we have experimented with all types of temporary shelters for the occasional bad-weather. What we have learned has been perfected into what is known in Mountain Men camp as "the art of tarpage." The camp's overall goals have always been to foster creativity, laughter and independence, as well as awareness of self, others and the environment. The use of creative tarpage helps our efforts to accomplish these goals.

On this June day, as we headed to Alaska, we were camped at Clayton Lake State Park. This oasis is in the rolling grasslands of northern New Mexico and is home to one of the world's most notable collections of dinosaur tracks. Scientists have dubbed this area part of Dinosaur Highway, a region running up through Colorado and Wyoming that is believed to have once been the western shore of an ancient ocean. The tracks likely belong to a group of dinosaurs known as Iguanodons, three-toed creatures some thirty feet in length. To see the prints is incredible. In addition, Clayton Lake is also a major respite for migratory birds traveling along the Rio Grande Flyway. On this particular lake, according to our ranger, over 4,000 Canada geese had congregated to take advantage of the rich aquatic environment and the protected calm waters of the lake basin.

Today the Mountain Men staff and I had just challenged the campers to form a dozen teams to produce a sleeping structure that met the criteria of being stable and functional within twenty minutes time. Each team of two boys was provided with the same materials: tarps, duct tape, mosquito netting, cots, twine and equal portions of PVC pipe and joints. The goal was to create a home for the night that would house two guys. Upon the proverbial "ready, set, go," the boys jumped into action to construct their home. Immediately, we noted a great variety of approaches—with teams exhibiting great creativity and problem-solving. Some boys, though, began to struggle due to conflicts in how best to approach things. Others worked smoothly right away as members exchanged suggestions and construction accelerated.

What did the homes look like? Everyone had the same exact materials list but produced very different structures. The winner was chosen and asked to provide an explanation to the group about the how and whys of their design. With great laughter, they boys circled up around the winner—a rectangular structure with a full covering of transparent mosquito netting held aloft by PVC pipes and secured in place by what else but duct tape, of course. "Our house meets all the requirements and is safe from the elements," one boy explained. "And it works!" Truly, it was practical, stable and offered an entrance and exit without destruction of the structure itself, and it had lots of room.

This exercise was repeated frequently throughout the trip, and by the time we reached Rock Creek, Montana, and still with many miles to go before Alaska, the young men had perfected "tarpage." They knew what materials they preferred and how best to put them together to build protective structures. Some even built creative tarpage condos, which allowed for card games to flourish completely protected from rain or wind.

Every adventure we take is unique, and so the staff always looks forward to seeing what's next along the trails of the young Mountain Men, in the evolving art of tarpage!

BUILDING YOUNG MEN: CREATIVITY

Hebrews 3:4 "For every house is built by someone, but God is the builder of everything."

The experience of building shelters daily on our travels up to Alaska and back may seem simplistic and of no importance. It may appear as merely a fun activity. Well, the process is great fun, but the learning experiences are truly invaluable. The boys have to decide what materials work best in what environments. They have to figure out how to put those materials together to achieve a satisfactory structure that will not collapse in rain or wind. They have to learn to work together. Numerous other complex challenges have to be overcome that require tapping into creativity, self-reliance and problem-solving capabilities. And, most important, this bustle of activity with tarps, duct tape, twine and PVC piping helps build a foundation for life-long confidence as a result of repeated challenges, failures, successes and ultimately accomplishments.

Consider the Boys in Your Life....

One of the most inherent characteristics of boys at any age is that they like to build forts. From an early age, they create forts out of anything they can find. This inherent creativity is hardwired. Take a look at your young man, big or small. It doesn't take much to build a fort for a young guy inside the living room or under the dining room table with sheets, blankets, chairs and the like. Or for a young teen, have him go outside and build a fort out in the backyard using household materials. And don't forget duct tape! Be sure to leave the electronics behind. You will see what fun can happen.

COUNTING COUP
Rabbit Ears Pass, Colorado 2003

"It is curious that physical courage should be so common in the world and moral courage so rare."
—Mark Twain

Mountain Man I is an amazing machine! Built exclusively for the purpose of travel-camping across America, the white bus with the blue stripe is no ordinary bus! On this summery day we challenged all of its ten gears and its coolant system. The bus climbed slowly up the side of the steep mountain pass exiting Steamboat Springs, Colorado, toward the top and our evening camp-site. I had been carefully watching the temperature gauge and was concerned because I had never seen the gauge reach this level of hot. The straight-line, six-cylinder diesel engine always ran cool.

Today was different. Low gears, engaged with maximum power, pitted us against gravity. Our 26,000-pound, fully loaded bus struggled up the seven degree grade on our way to the summit. We hoped we wouldn't blow something. In all the travels of the Mountain Men, in all the roads we've covered in the western United States and Canada, this particular mountain is by far the most challenging. Finally, after twenty, white-knuckle minutes, we reached the summit and eased over into the valley known as Rabbit Ears Pass. At 9,426 feet above sea level, the pass straddles the Continental Divide separating the Pacific and Atlantic watersheds. The young men cheered our accomplishment. And they immediately noticed a mountain formation across the valley called Rabbit Ears Peak, so-named by early beaver trappers, which certainly does look like a pair of rabbit ears sticking up in the distance. Around it unfolded a majestic expanse of Colorado's natural high country beauty.

Now safely gliding comfortably through the valley, we looked for a campsite. Soon we found an attractive location along the edge of a grove of towering spruce and pine trees and pulled over, a gorgeous, mountain meadowland before us. This region is one of the lushest regions of Colorado, boasting few people but great diversity of wildlife including huge numbers of deer, elk and pronghorn antelope. The local flora attracts a wide range of birds and more than a dozen species of butterflies. There are woodpeckers, green-headed towhees and even the tiny Saw-whet owl. Fields of orange, red and yellow wildflowers burst with color.

The boys spilled out of the bus and grabbed cots, sleeping bags and tarpage equipment in preparation for setting up their home base. Overseeing the camp set-up, the staff would occasionally see a young man stop and simply gaze out across the overpowering beauty of the natural landscape. This is what our camp is all about. These experiences are about being in the moment—that rare time when a boy's senses are fully open, and he is experiencing heightened awareness.

He is appreciating life and nature without distraction. Such observation never ceases to bring a smile to every staff member as they
themselves appreciate the knowledge of what they are witnessing in
young men.

Our campers carry the name Mountain Men for several reasons.
We spend as much time as possible exploring the Rocky Mountains,
and we teach history of the country's early westward expansion.
Our instruction often includes visits to the locations of key, historical events offering direct revelations into the interactions between
Native People and American explorers between 1804 and the late
1880s, the era of the Mountain Men.

Earlier in the day, the campers had experienced some of those
key events. Along the way they had watched Kevin Costner's *Dances
with Wolves*, the mostly accurate portrayal of the Plains Indian conflicts during the 1860's between the U.S. Calvary and the Lakota
Sioux. In the film, as in real life, there were depictions of how Indian
warriors demonstrated courage and gained honor. The tribes had created a system to distinguish themselves between rival members, thus
showing who was the most honorable and the most courageous. And
the many benefits within the social structure included leadership
positions and preferred choice of mates.

The system of gaining honor through courage was called
"counting coup." What was involved? In counting coup, a warrior had
to get close enough to his enemies to physically touch or strike them.
It was considered to be one of the highest acts of courage amongst
warriors. To be in close proximity demonstrated superiority over the
enemy and imparted humiliation, and it elevated the warrior's position within his tribe. Surprisingly, during this brutal time, showing
courage was valued more highly than killing one's enemy. The best

way to affect a coup, and at great personal risk, was to charge one's enemy directly and strike them with a hand, a weapon or a coup-stick. Very young boys were taught this practice through games before their rite of passage into manhood made them warriors. Over time counting coup became an institutionalized practice. In fact, during the last stages of the Plains Indian Wars, counting coup was used at the Battle of the Little Bighorn when Custer's ill-fated plans led to massacre of the 7th Calvary Regiment by the combined forces of the Lakota, Northern Cheyenne and Arapaho tribes.

So now, with a slight sharpness in the late afternoon breeze, the boys were rambunctious and ready to play. Our plan was to have a coup-war among the tribe of young Mountain Men. Talk about excited! The boys were jumping up and down with anticipation. We explained the rules for safety, including what could or could not be used for coup-sticks and how the game would unfold and so on. The most highly prized coup would be a strike by the hand. Once everyone understood the rules, the twenty-one campers formed their own tribes, three in all. We gave them another fifteen minutes to architect their strategies and pick out their preferred locations in the meadow.

If ever you have had the good fortune to witness complete creativity and anticipation in groups of boys then you would recognize the sight the staff beheld that afternoon. The game was totally unfamiliar, the area unfamiliar and what might happen unfamiliar—all ingredients that make a game fun for boys! Finally, the time for battle arrived. I gave the order for the boys to go to their preferred starting point. Some headed into the forest; others gathered nearby. Next a sharp whistle, and the game was on!

Running wildly, screaming like the Native People heard in the movie, the boys raced all over! The staff was trying to count coup for each team as someone would tap a competitor and then dart off. Whooping and yelling, laughing hysterically, jumping over skunk cabbage patches, charging then avoiding one another, the boys zig-zagged about in mock battle for a good twenty minutes. When fatigue began to appear, I called the game over, yelling "DONE!"

Back at the camp site, everyone circled up, some standing, some sitting. We announced the results. A couple of guys with a significant number of individual coups began strutting around, the most coura-geous of the tribe! No one really cared who was a winner as everyone had experienced a total blast. They had burned off energy and lived out history based upon real events from the Plains Indian Wars. That night around campfire, a near-full moon above us, the discussion centered around the lifestyle of the Plains Indians. Everything you could imagine was discussed. Where did the Indians come from? How many tribes were there? How did they get horses? How did they hunt? And, of course, who dreamed up coup? On and on the talks went until only embers remained in our fire and sleepy boys finally retired to their cots, tired and happy to sleep under the stars.

It was a peaceful ending to another day of adventure and learning with the Mountain Men.

BUILDING YOUNG MEN: MORAL COURAGE

1 Corinthians 16:13 "Be on your guard; stand firm in the faith; be men of courage; be strong."

Physical courage among men is highly valued in today's modern world. That is evident in our fascination with the sports industry. Estimated by the International Association of Sports Economists, in 2008, to be between a $44 and $73 billion dollar a year industry, sports are the main way courage is demonstrated in America today. Competition, that's what it's all about, or is it? A player willing to sacrifice himself so his team can win is considered valiant. We play out our admiration of physical courage by watching televised events and participating in live events. These days we demonstrate our courage to others through increasingly bizarre methods. Consider the proliferation of extreme sports: BASE jumping off buildings and bridges, bungee jumping, wingsuit flying, skydiving and Everest-type mountain climbing, all make what used to be a big thrill, like whitewater rafting, seem mild. Today the list of things a person can do to get an adrenaline high and demonstrate physical courage is endless.

And yet isn't moral courage what's really important?

Consider the Boys in Your Life....

Boys, especially in adolescence, love to demonstrate their prowess and physical courage in competition with others. This is part of growing up. If there is not at least an element of danger and the possibility of injury, blood or an accident, then they are not as interested in the activity. This is just how it is! Do not be fearful of this characteristic in boys.

But what about real courage, moral courage? This is the highest character value in life. Sadly, most civilized societies today are awash in moral lawlessness. So as we consider our youth, it is vital to consider questions about moral courage. Where does it come from? Of what value is it in a successful life? And how is moral courage different from physical courage? How do we nurture both? After thinking about this yourself, try discussing examples of the differences of each in his life. Try to distinguish what is and is not moral courage. Try focusing on stories that involve sacrifice of self to the service of others. If you look, there are plenty of examples. See what your boy comes up with, you will be encouraged!

OUR CANVAS

Yellowstone National Park, June 2003

"Nature is the art of God."
– Dante Alighieri

The Mountain Men were at one of the seven wonders of North America: Yellowstone National Park. Established in 1872 as America's first national park through an act of the U.S. Congress and signed into law by President Ulysses S. Grant, Yellowstone remains the poster child of our parks system. Blue skies, wildflowers everywhere, birds aplenty, all life seems happy to be alive. The boys were content, too. Why not? In the middle of a summer adventure, on a road-trip through some of the country's most scenic and exciting territory, they felt the joys of a good life grounded in nature. They had seen the Grand Canyon of the Yellowstone River, hiked through hundreds of geysers, walked within feet of buffalo, elk, deer and coyotes. They had seen eagles and ospreys, caught rainbow and brown trout in the Firehole River and marveled at Yellowstone's incredible beauty.

Just as we were leaving the park that Sunday in June, heading east toward Cody, Wyoming, I spotted a favorite pullout. I headed into it and parked the bus. "Out of the bus guys!" I hollered from the driver's seat. "Head up onto that ridge and have a seat anywhere you like."

Boys piled out, talking and laughing. They climbed up the steep hill and then marveled at the view. Twenty-three of us gazed west across the snow-covered Absaroka Range and into the heart of the Yellowstone Country. Guys were clearly contemplating nature at its finest. "Today is Sunday, the Lord's day," I said. "Let's take a few minutes to reflect about our lives. I would like to share some thoughts with you guys about life, our place in it and our responsibilities."

The young men all listened intently. The air carried a sweet smell of wildflowers. Birds flitted about the meadow and within nearby pine trees, while hawks and eagles soared effortlessly higher up in the mountain skies. The views of the Wapiti Valley were simply incredible. I said: "Guys, take a look before you. Take in the colors, the wildness, the beauty. All around us we can see, feel, smell and touch the magnificence of the beauty of God's handiwork in nature. Isn't it spectacular?" They all nodded affirmatively.

"As you look out over this magnificent valley, consider the picture you see before you as a canvas, a painting if you will," I continued. "God painted this picture for us as He did the entire world we live in. Not only did He fill it with natural beauty, but with unbelievable varieties of life including people. As you think about this I want you to consider your life right now, both here in the moment and in your life back home. Now consider your life as a canvas and yourself as an artist. How are you painting your life? Are you adding delicate and deliberate colors and dimension through careful brush strokes that compliment yourself and those around you? Are you blending your skills and gifts into service to God, your family and others? Or are you now simply throwing paint against the canvas with no thought of a plan or design, just going through the motions based upon your own desires? Think about that for a moment."

I was then silent for two or three minutes, then continued. "When we go forward today from this spot, I want you to remember this view across the valley. Remember it as you are growing up; remember what kind of picture you are painting. People see the canvas of your life as you paint it. Will they see kindness or hostility, gentleness or anger, sharing and caring or selfishness, moral courage or weakness? Will they see integrity and honesty or deceit and insincerity? Each of us gets a choice how we live each day of our lives. Be aware of your choices. Choose to respond rather than react to situations and do the right thing. Choose to paint a masterpiece with your life."

We lingered for a few moments longer as I prayed for the boys, their families and our adventure together. We then rose to return to the bus. Boys ran laughing and joyful down the hillside to reboard Mountain Man I for Cody, primed for the next adventure!

BUILDING YOUNG MEN: CHARACTER

Ephesians 6:4 "Fathers, do not exasperate your children; instead, bring them up in the training and instruction of the Lord."

As we strive to help our young men grow into strong, capable and grounded adults, character development is often what challenges us most. Our own lives are difficult, and kids can be daunting, especially in adolescence. But as a parent you are the most influential person in your child's life. Did you ever consider that his teachers may be spending more time daily with him than you? Sounds impossible? Each teacher devotes approximately 45 minutes a day with your child. They read your child's moods, frustrations and joys, all while imparting knowledge. These days, when most kids go home, one or both parents are still at work. There is dinner in some fashion, hopefully some study and then bed.

Think about your situation. How much one-on-one time do you spend together each day? Hopefully, more than his teachers.

Consider the Boys in Your Life....

To build character, it is critical that you make time daily to coach, counsel, love and listen to your children. Such practices will bring them security and a willingness to listen to you in the future when things might get rough. This is because you have already invested in building a foundation of trust.

One of the best methodologies to build character is based on deliberate and consistent intent and actions. Everything should be focused on the end result. So do you have a deliberate, consistent plan for your son? Do you follow the plan or is life getting in the way? Time and intent are your allies. You can get started right away by discussing the concept of a life canvas. Here is an opportunity: get some colored pencils or finger paints. Sit down together and, depending upon age, have him actually draw or even finger paint his life. You do the same and then compare canvases. You will be amazed at the insights you both will gain.

CHAPTER 10 — THE NEED TO BELONG

WOLF DYNAMICS

Somewhere in the Rocky Mountains – Summer 2012

"We are driven by five genetic needs: survival, love and belonging, power, freedom, and fun."

—William Glasser

The Mountain Men of the 1800s were often solitary. As trappers they worked the rivers of the West in search of beaver to trade for cash, goods or services. These men were tough, hardened by all sorts of challenges from a largely unexplored territory—threats from nasty weather, Indian tribes, grizzly bear, cougars, wolves, snakes and a whole host of biting insects. Loneliness too, was a fact of life. There were no grocery stores or Walmarts for supplies; no hot showers or easy-to-buy meals. Everything they used was made by their own hand or brought from towns before the trapping seasons started.

And when the seasons ended, they would head down the mountains with their furs to join annual spring and summer gatherings hosted by large trapping companies. Most of these rendezvous, or trading fairs, were in what is known today as Wyoming, then the Oregon Country, on Snake or Shoshone Indian tribal territory. They were lively events with singing, music and dancing, shooting and knife-throwing contests and card games. Thus, the rendezvous offered men not only a pay day for their furs, but a distraction from the hardness of trapping. It was a time to congregate, share stories, experiences, skills and ideas. Many business deals and arrangements that led to future exploration of the West were completed in these rendezvous between the traders, Mountain Men, Indians, eastern businessmen and the military.

Just like the Mountain Men of old, men today crave interaction. This is why social media has become so popular. Though society may paint men as manly only if they are strong and independent, all people, boys included, require interaction for mental and emotional health. And yet technological connections are greatly flawed. Texting disavows the intonation and inflection of the voice, offers no facial expressions and often shortens the message through acronyms. Email produces a similar effect. Cellular phones have evolved to include pictures and video, but let's be realistic: the only true communication is face to face.

For young modern-day Mountain Men, here's where the dynamics of a wolf pack are noteworthy. For example, research by scientist David Mech shows that wolves live in families; moreover, they are not born leaders or followers as earlier research suggested. Wolf parents are just raising their offspring while the offspring are just following the parents as would young in most other species. As a camp, we explore the places of the former Mountain Men, traveling throughout the western United States, Canada and Alaska. Along the way we witness the dynamics of a wolf pack forming within our camp. The boys are following the leaders and playing together along the way. At first, the boys who know each other will chat and group together while the others are generally shy and solitary. Eventually the solitary boys will migrate into the group to share a few experiences. Within two days, the dynamics change. New groups form and the solitary boys are no longer evident. It is awesome to see how communal meals, group activities and campfires at night can meld a group of young men together as a pack.

As the days progress, the boys move through clearly identifiable stages of community. Within a week of sleeping outside every night under the stars, these young men emerge from the cover of technology. They move into a natural biorhythm of going to bed after campfire and rising with the sun. Now the real boy emerges, his true personality evident. Boys play again and make up games, chasing, running, laughing and exploring. Communications evolve into deeper conversations. Questioning everything, they compare ideas and reflect upon their lives and experiences.

The young Mountain Men have become a wolf pack, and the adventure of learning is now in full swing.

BUILDING YOUNG MEN: THE NEED TO BELONG

Psalm 133:1. "How good and pleasant it is when brothers live together in unity!"

Belonging is natural and fundamental to our sense of happiness, security and well-being. In a recent article in *Psychology Today* entitled "In The Name of Love," Dr. Aaron Ben-Zeev, a philosopher and former president of the University of Haifa, highlights the important work of psychologists Roy Baumeister and Mark Leary: "Individuals need to form and maintain a minimum amount of lasting, positive and significant, interpersonal relationships. This need is accomplished through frequent and positive interactions with the same individuals within a long-term, stable and caring environment."

Adolescence presents this key human need—reminiscent of a wolf pack dynamic—in remarkable and dramatic fashion. If you haven't spent time in a middle or high school lately, you should consider volunteering or substituting a few short days. Watch what is happening. In an effort to belong kids gravitate to others in order to gain a sense of acceptance. Usually they share common interests with the chosen group, thus facilitating communication and interaction. So ask the kids the names of the groups in school and which ones they are part of.

Another way to think about the need for human belonging is that it is the opposite of loneliness and isolation. No mentally healthy person wishes to be lonely. Now consider that your child's school is his or her primary community. This is the major influence on belief structures, values and decisions. Be involved and know what is going on. Meet and build a relationship with your child's teachers. And consider what Dr. Brene Brown of the University of Houston says about belonging, in the development of individual identity: "Those who have a strong sense of love and belonging have the courage to be imperfect." We might also add, "as we all are."

Certainly none of us are perfect. Therefore we all need a sense of love and belonging in order to have the courage to become who we are meant to be. Imperfect as we are, the goal is to get better!

Consider the Boys in Your Life....

What "packs" or groups is your boy involved in? Are you guiding his direction with respect to his passions, abilities and skills? How much of his communication is obtained from technology versus first-person interactions? Take a look and consider how face-to-face communication may be improved at home and in his life. For example, talk with your kids and express your interest in them. Tell them how much you love them and wish to communicate with them. Introduce the idea of tech-free zones and what that might look like for your family. Together, talk about advantages of the idea. Agree on times and places in the home—like at dinner, in the car, etc.—where everyone agrees that no technology devices will be used. Let them try and set the boundaries where the only communications and entertainment will be between each other. Try it out. Have dinner together at the table tonight. Talk. Laugh. Plan some outdoor family-pack activities together minus electronics. See what happens.

Chapter 11 — Service

The Playscape

Petersburg, Alaska, 2008

"I do not know what your destiny will be, but one thing I know: the only ones among you who will be really happy are those who will have sought and found how to serve."

—Albert Schweitzer

At 12:40 a.m., our ferry slowly angled toward the harbor of Petersburg, Alaska. Sleepy boys gathered in the front observation deck where we had agreed to meet to take a headcount prior to disembarking. All was dark, silent and smooth this clear night, and shimmering stars were so bright at this latitude that they looked fake and close enough to touch. As we approached the dock the captain performed an amazing parallel parking maneuver for the 400-foot ferry, sliding the boat precisely into the gangplank. My staff soon headed the boys up the plank and into the terminal. Meantime, I went below deck and fired up our bus, Mountain Man I. Grady, our faithful camp dog, who had been sleeping in the back bus lounge, came forward happy to see me. As I spun up the machine, Grady pushed his head under my arm and across my leg, content to be part of the group again.

Once safely ashore, I gathered everyone and began to look for our host, the principal of the Petersburg Schools. There he was in his white pickup, despite the late hour. But when we did our head count, I discovered we were one boy short. A second count, still short. Quickly, the missing boy was identified. Regretfully, and with embarrassment, I exited the bus, told the principal the situation and then sprinted to the ferry where I informed a deck mate. Immediately, they began a search and thirty minutes later a sleepy, blond-haired boy walked up the gangplank. He had merely fallen asleep. Soon after his fellow campers expanded his nickname of "Piano Man" (he was a gifted piano player) to "Stowaway Piano Man."

We finally settled into the school for the night. I thanked our host for his gracious hospitality, extending an invitation to breakfast. He said he would come by in the morning then departed to get some sleep in what remained of his evening. It is really something to stop and consider the welcoming spirit of Alaskans. This man had never before met me until thirty minutes earlier, and he had just handed me the keys to the high school gymnasium. His willingness to help our camp was based upon a thirty-minute phone call months earlier and a few emails. Everything was based on trust; this town leader had responsibility to protect the interests of the community of Petersburg... and he had placed his trust in me. His trust was based upon his love for kids and his understanding of our camp. Indeed, in this last frontier, in a harsh and unforgiving environment, man is not at the top of the food chain so people here understand the challenges and just naturally help each other out. What a wonderful experience to learn that not everyone has become conditioned to distrust and fear one another. This lesson helped to demonstrate to our boys how relationships can and should start. As a result, our boys felt valued and wanted to live up to our host's high expectations by pleasing him with good behavior, which each of them did admirably.

Morning found us extremely hungry. Our crew of thirty-three plowed through ten pounds of bacon, sixty eggs and two loaves of bread on the first pass. And when the principal showed up, I brought up our practice of providing service to the towns we visit. "It teaches boys about service and giving back to communities that host us," I explained. "Do you have any ideas of how we might help out Petersburg during our visit?"

"Why don't you visit the village chamber of commerce and see what they might suggest," he said.

As morning began to unfurl the boys reveled in their new environment. They were mesmerized by the bald eagles screeching their annoyance at us from the tops of neighboring spruce trees. Not just one eagle but dozens! As we got our bearings we could see down the hillside directly to the ocean and the pier just three blocks away. Fishing vessels lined the docks. We gathered the boys, offered some basic instructions and then told them to head into town to explore. Lunch would be back at camp. Groups of guys immediately took off into town, free to look around, learn and be boys. Imagine the feelings of freedom! The only rules to follow were clear: treat everyone you meet with the utmost courtesy and respect, do nothing that would bring embarrassment to yourself or the camp, and have fun!

Meanwhile, I asked my assistant Nicholas Cowey to head down to the Petersburg Chamber of Commerce and see if he could find a project for us. "I'm on it," he said with a big smile. "I'll be back soon." And before I knew it, he and everyone else had returned.

Nicholas shared his news with the crew: "Well, on the ferry arriving before us, the community received a shipment of recycled rubber chips to be used to build a playscape. It's already been delivered. The woman down at the chamber thinks they could use some help putting it in."

"Perfect, let's see what's going on," I said.

Nicholas and I climbed into the Mountain Man bus and headed up along a narrow road. Near the town baseball and soccer fields we saw a man with a shovel slinging rubber chips across an expansive playground. We pulled up, stepped out and introduced ourselves. I explained that we were looking for a service project and had a group of young men ready to lend their helping hands. His face lit up. "My name is Tom," he said. "Man, I could sure use your help! It's just me, and it will probably take me all day and then some to get this crate of rubber spread out."

His eyes paused on our white bus with the elk antlers. "We're an adventure camp for boys," I told him. "Alaska represents the biggest adventure most of us will ever experience." Tom cheerfully welcomed us to his state and asked if we could return at 1:00 p.m. so he would have time to round up a bunch of rakes and shovels. We agreed and then jumped back on Mountain Man I for the short trip back to the school.

After lunch, replete with sandwiches and gallons of lemonade, bags of chips, bags of cookies and yet more sandwiches, we circled up the campers to talk more about the concept of service. "I want each of you to think about a time when someone helped you personally or helped someone in your family or when you witnessed an act of selfless service to others," I suggested. For fifteen minutes we heard incredible stories. Contrary to many prevailing views, young men will gladly open up about themselves and their experiences.

We then loaded up the Mountain Man bus, including our dog Grady, and headed again up along the narrow road. This time we spotted Tom atop a John Deere tractor with a forklift attachment secured to the front end. Underneath the forklift was a huge wooden crate of color rubber chips. Each boy walked up to Tom to introduce himself and shake hands. He thanked them enthusiastically. "Grab a shovel or rake," he said. "I'll dump the rubberized chips into the play-scape using the tractor and you guys can spread them across the area."

Surprisingly, by 2:30 p.m., we were done! It's incredible what more than two dozen teenage boys can accomplish. Not only that but they laughed and chased each other, and when finished, they climbed around on the playscape… just being boys. As for "Stowaway Piano Man," this camper was one of the hardest workers, almost as if trying to make up for his sleepy mischief.

There is no greater opportunity or investment for men, young or old, than that of selfless service. Our young Mountain Men per-formed cheerfully, willingly and admirably. Everyone felt the warm satisfaction and pride of accomplishment of a contribution made entirely for the benefit of others.

When we finished our work and our play, off we went looking for another adventure, which turned out to be some late afternoon fishing for salmon at Eagle Roost Park.

BUILDING YOUNG MEN: SERVICE

Galatians 6:10 "Therefore, as we have opportunity,
let us do good to all people, especially to those who
belong to the family of believers."

Altruism, or the concept of selflessness, has been debated among psychologists for years relative to whether it actually exists or not. Whether we are hardwired for generosity or whether we have to learn it doesn't really matter; it's the act of service to others that matters. According to a 2012 article in *U.S. News & World Report*, "Why Helping Others Makes Us Happy," Phillip Moeller reviews the reality of helping others. It turns out that people who volunteer have higher self-esteem, experience greater levels of happiness and develop more positive psychological well-being than those of us who do not. Moreover, feelings of connectedness go up, helping us meet that most innate need, that of connection and belonging.

Interestingly, the United States has one of the highest rates of volunteerism in the world. Research shows that even people who are forced to volunteer benefit from the experiences. Studies of at-risk children have shown they develop a more positive self-concept and produce higher grades in school; in turn, this contributes to lower pregnancy rates, drop-out rates and use of illegal drugs. Helping others while in high school also results in more volunteerism as an adult. Studies show this consistency of volunteering contributes to consistency of the positive result factors already noted. The main reasons people volunteer are actually due to the products they receive from the experiences: values development, community concern, esteem enhancement, understanding of others and personal development.

Of particular note is the huge upswing over the last fifteen years in vacation volunteerism. Organizations like EarthWatch, Globe Aware and other similar non-profits have seen increases in participation upwards of 40 percent. EarthWatch helps volunteers connect with opportunities doing scientific research on environmental topics, and Globe Aware promotes cultural awareness and sustainability; volunteers working side by side with people in developing nations so they can stand on their own two feet. Clearly, many people today are beginning to use their vacation time not to play or relax from the hectic, high-speed world we live in, but rather to give of themselves and help others. How encouraging!

What we do know for certain is simply this: helping others helps everyone, especially the volunteer!

Consider the Boys in Your Life....

Service and sharing are critical lessons in character-building. How are the boys in your life doing? What learning opportunities have you intentionally provided? One of the best ways to accomplish character building is to lead by your own example. Try volunteering together; that's more meaningful than just telling boys what should be done. Your young man can help you do whatever you have arranged. Later, have a quiet conversation about the experience. You will be encouraged as will your boy and both of you will be closer.

ZODIACAL LIGHT

McDonald Observatory, Fort Davis, Texas, June 2013

"God created everything by number, weight and measure."

— Sir Isaac Newton

A s the crowd gathered in the circular, outdoor amphitheater, a palpable murmur of excitement could be heard. The interest was being generated by our unique location and the upcoming presentation. The sky was remarkably clear this evening as the Earth rotated gently from civil into nautical twilight. These terms refer to the position below the horizon the Sun appears to drop as we rotate and is marked by increasing six degree increments. The Mountain Men, along with a hundred or so others, were sitting atop Mount Locke in Texas, at an elevation of 6,790 feet, and looking into some of the country's clearest and darkest skies. We were attending what the University of Texas McDonald Observatory facility calls a "Star Party," an engaging opportunity to learn some astronomy.

Looking about the night sky we could see an amazing panorama of telescopes on the mountain tops. The magnificent Hobby-Eberly telescope was off to the north end of the observatory property. One of the five largest optical telescopes in the world, the Hobby-Eberly was originally designed in 1966 as a spectroscopic survey telescope. Recent enhancements have allowed focused research into what scientists call dark energy. Today Hobby-Eberly is leading the charge into investigations about this mysterious energy, which most scientists agree must exist in order for the universe to continue its expansion—a phenomena currently verified by observation of light behaviors from astronomical objects within the universe.

So many unknowns continue to baffle us, but one thing we are pretty sure of is that the universe appears to be of infinite dimension. How is that possible? It seems our situation currently is one wherein the more data we obtain, the more questions that arise. Maybe this realization of more learning producing more questions is what brought Sir Isaac Newton and other scientists to their conclusions about God.

As the skies continued to darken about us, we looked across the field to see the louvers of the massive Hobby-Eberly begin to open. They open in order to equalize the inside and outside temperatures of the telescope facility so as to minimize the bending of light waves entering the scope. Such temperature equalization of air serves to provide the sharpest imaging of objects as possible. After the louvers fully opened we turned our attention back to the western sky. We began to notice an unusual apparition developing before us. A massive, triangular cone of strange and glowing ethereal light began to appear, extending up from the horizon perhaps forty-five to sixty degrees at its peak point and then widening downward until it disappeared into a purple, black mountain range.

"Do you know what that light is?" asked our presenter, a resident researcher at the observatory. He used a powerful, green laser pointer to direct our attention toward the glowing object.

Someone called out a guess, "The lights of El Paso?"

"A very good guess but incorrect," he replied. Several other suggestions followed. "The light you are seeing is known as the Zodiacal Light," he said finally. "This light is a reflection of the sun off of particles in space that remain from the very beginning of the universe. Imagine that. We are lucky tonight. Atmospheric conditions have to be just right so it's unusual to see."

The campers marveled at seeing such a phenomena. "Seeing this light is really cool," said one boy thoughtfully. The other campers agreed. And while scientists love to speculate, investigate, argue, publish and present new knowledge about the findings on the universe (as well as every other field of study imaginable), the bottom line today is that no one really knows much about the origin of the universe or dark energy. Geologists tell us the world is 4.6 billion years old, based upon scientific dating of rocks. Astronomers tell us the universe is continuing to expand today having begun its outward trajectory at the moment of inception commonly referred to as the Big Bang. Biologists tell us there are approximately 8.7 million species of plant and animal life on Earth....

These conclusions are in reality, educated guesses based upon observations, extrapolations and opinions. This is why the unanswered ideas remain theories instead of facts or laws. We don't really know.

What then do we know about the existence of God? Can we see Him; can we experience him? Does he exist? Throughout time, people have considered this question of creation. Believers and atheists continue to debate creation and the existence of God. As a scientist myself, I would suggest to you that based upon the statistics of probability alone it is impossible for God not to exist. Another consideration I offer comes from work with kids. Kids can "see" reality easier than most adults. For example, over the years I have had more than one discussion with kids that went something like this. "So," asks a young man, "if all life on Earth evolved, where did the Earth come from?" I answer, "Current theories of many scientists suggest that asteroids struck each other over billions of years in space eventually forming the Earth." "Well," says the young man, "then where did the asteroids come from?" "From the Big Bang," says I. "Well then," asks the young man, "What caused the Big Bang?" "Excellent question, the truth is no one knows," I reply. "Hmm," the young man utters.

"Well, what about life on Earth?" he asks again. I respond, "Again, many scientists believe that life evolved from molecules in the oceans." The boy looks at me and continues, "Then where did the molecules that make up the oceans come from?" I keep answering, "Many believe that the water on Earth came from comets, asteroids and from out-gassing produced by volcanism during the early days of Earth. The elements and molecules that formed under tremendous heat and pressure during the Big Bang arrived by way of asteroid collisions." The boy looks at me and then realizes where the conversation is headed. He asks finally, "So, what caused the Big Bang and where did the original atoms come from to make the asteroids, the planets, the stars and the water and the molecules that came together to make the DNA that evolved into life on Earth?" "Very good questions! No one knows," I say. Truly and simply, out of the mouths of babes comes amazing reasoning and logic.

Beyond statistics, logic and various forms of reasoning, one can simply look at the amazing realities of men's experiences with God over recorded time. We see historical and archeological records of God and his people. We experience answered prayers, miracles, divine appointments and the written word that offers us a path of spiritual physics to follow. Spiritual physics refers to the realities of boundaries, responsibilities and understandings of the word of God given to us to help us follow the trail to Christ. Those spiritual laws also exist to guide us to positive interactions between ourselves and with God. Like the world of the scientist who investigations are based upon the laws of matter and motion in the natural world, these spiritual laws define reality of what we see happening as well as what we do not see. Combined, these spiritual and natural physics laws provide compelling evidence for a rational man to realize he has a maker who is real.

Tonight had offered our camp of Mountain Men a remarkable opportunity, plunging us into the magnificence, beauty, mystery and incomprehensibility of the universe. We were presented a challenge to consider our place in the universe as our lives here on Earth unfold. There exists nothing like the outdoors to present a person with an introspection of themselves and their place in the world, especially from a guided tour of the universe atop Mount Locke.

BUILDING YOUNG MEN: GOD IS REAL

Genesis 1:1. "In the beginning God created the heavens and the earth."

The mystery of creation continues to challenge us as it has since the beginning of recorded time. As humans, we simply must know truth and to obtain truth we must have irrefutable evidence in order to be sure of what we know. Hence, we seek knowledge through a process we know as science. Based upon observation and measurement, hypothesis and experimentation, all of our knowledge of the natural world has been generated through science. Some scientists embrace atheism. They tell us there is no God and that we have all evolved out of a primordial soup.

And yet, consider this: we exist in a precise location, Earth, within a seemingly infinite universe that allows liquid water in abundance on a planet with a temperature range and atmosphere that is perfect for life and held in place by a satellite moon without which we could not exist. Atheists argue there is no proof of the existence of God. In fact, some leading current day scientists have said that science makes God unnecessary. Interesting perspective. Consider that we can't see dark matter or wind and yet believe that both exist. Consider that once we could not see atoms yet predicted they not only existed but in fact could be split producing enormous amounts of energy—as happened with atomic energy weapon technology in the early 1940s. This nuclear idea turned out to be correct, but for the longest time it was based upon inferred, indirect evidence through mathematical calculations and extrapolation.

Science is fascinating and ever more unfolding with tons of new data. It is this data, claimed as irrefutable evidence, that has resulted in heated debates between creationists and evolutionists for years now. The bottom line is everyone wants to know how and where did we come from. Recall the young man's questions earlier, and then consider that science and creation make wonderfully compatible partners.

Consider the Boys in Your Life....

Every man and woman contemplates the origin of their existence. How did I get here? Why am I here? Is there a God? These questions are of particular interest to young men going through the introspection period of adolescence and early adulthood. They often do not yet have enough life experiences that allow them to fully analyze how life and God work with mankind. Boys need lots of guidance, attention and affirmation in order to become successful men.

A suggestion: take time to ponder the heavens above. Check the moon phase then plan a time and go find a lightless environment, Together with your young man consider the magnitude of the universe and then talk with him about his thoughts. Ask him how is it possible that all of what we see, hear, feel, taste, touch and smell could possibly be? Share the evidence you know of God. Later, follow up and show him scriptures and explain how they are related and that all of the prophecies presented thousands of years ago (before technology) have come true relative to the life of Christ. Teach him the history and reasoning of both science and religion. Develop a focused faith practice with him.

If you do this, God will bless you both. Your relationship will deepen. Your young man will see the connections between old and new, and he will have an opportunity at introspection, growth, maturity and leadership that will help him grow into a man of sound reason and faith in our Lord.

THE FIAT CONCEPT
Zion National Park, Utah, June 2007

" Never spend your money before you have it."

—Thomas Jefferson

On this particular adventure, one of our Mountain Men had quite a bit of financial backing. He was one of the younger guys, merely twelve, and had demonstrated extreme generosity to his fellow campers throughout the trip. He bought this or that, sharing his money and purchases. When coached by staff that he might want to hang onto some of his funds for the future he dismissed the idea. "All I have to do is call home," he had said. "Dad will give me more money."

As we headed for Zion National Park in Utah, another week of camp still remaining, he suddenly realized that he was bankrupt. No money remained in his pockets or in his account in the Bank of the Mountains, the name for our safe box where we kept boys' deposits of cash. He asked the staff if he could call his home in Florida. During a fuel stop, we let him call home. He came back really frustrated and told a staff member, "Dad said I couldn't have any more money!"

"How much did you start with?" I asked.

Very matter of factly, he said, "$300." That amount is really at the outside of what we had ever heard for a boy on our adventures and certainly a lot of money for someone so young. I told him, "How about I call your dad and talk to him. Would that be okay?"

"Yeah!" he said really excited. "That would be great. Thanks!"

I am certain that the young man thought my call would be to convince his dad to pony up some more cash so the fun could continue. During a free moment, I made a call to Florida and talked to his dad. We talked about the management of money, the choices for banking that the Mountain Men have, etc. The father explained that he did not want to continue supporting his son's frivolous expenditures. He asked what my thoughts were. I reminded him again about our banking system for the campers which is intended to embrace stewardship, discipline and accountability. "In these cases, learning the reality of bankruptcy in a safe environment where a young man won't go hungry, won't be left without shelter and will continue to participate in all of the activities is sometimes one of the greatest lessons in camp," I said. "What I suggest is for us to offer your son a job in order for him to earn money for the remainder of the week. How would you feel about that approach?"

"I think it is a great idea," said the dad. "What sort of job would you propose?"

"We have all sorts of opportunities to earn income," I said. "For example, washing the Mountain Man bus windshield each day pays $2.00. Washing and cleaning the inside and outside of all the bus windows pays $8.00 so there is $10.00 a day right there. We have other work, from kitchen and equipment cleaning to inventory of food stuffs. There is no shortage of work opportunities."

"Can you explain to him that we talked, and he is now employed by the Mountain Men under your direction?" asked Dad. "This is a terrific idea for learning."

"Sure. Glad to do it," I responded.

I planned to talk to the Florida youngster at the Zion National Park campgrounds when the windshield would be in optimum need for cleaning. Now, nearing our destination, I looked in the long rear view mirror to check on the boys. Lots of laughter, some ear buds in, music no doubt rocking them along, others reading, some napping in the lounge in the back. I then noticed two young men exchanging money. I called back to my staffer Nicholas Cowey and asked him to come forward. "Not sure what's up," I said, "but I noticed money being passed around and wondered if you could quietly check it out?"

On our trips the young men often play card games. Sometimes older guys use chips, but I had never seen money change hands. It has been my practice to allow slack reins but with an understanding that there *are* reins and *are* limits, always. When Nicholas returned he said, "You will never believe what the guys are doing!"

"Well, lay it on me," I said smiling. "What are they up to?"

"The older guys have discovered capitalism and the world of the entrepreneur," he replied. "Seems as though some of the younger kids are either running low on cash or bankrupt. The older guys actually formed a corporation with executives, accountants and sales people."

"Amazing. What are they selling?"

"That's the interesting part," he continued. "Whenever we stop for fuel, the older boys go into the store, pool their money and buy a bag of cookies or whatever they think might look appetizing to the younger kids. Then later on, when everyone wants snacks, they produce the desired goodies. The sale comes when a single cookie or a few cookies are sold for a profit. The members can then split the profits and plan the next sale."

"This is a great opportunity for us to teach our next financial lesson," I told Nicholas.

As I drove through Zion's canyons I marveled at how well the older boys had figured out the basics of the free enterprise system. They had identified a market opportunity, created a purchasing and distribution network, addressed sales, cost management, profit-sharing and expansion. They had, however, missed the fundamentals of our intent on the trip; we were trying to teach stewardship, sharing and accountability for each other.

The next morning before the hike into the fabulous Narrows of Zion's canyons, Nicholas and I addressed the campers and discussed the concept of "fiat money." We explained that fiat money means the use of virtually worthless paper money that is assigned value only as a result of a promise of faith that our government will honor at an agreed upon value. It has no intrinsic value like gold or silver. We discussed the use of money from the earliest days of recorded history when men used to barter for goods and services based upon trading things of value. We continued the discussion into the days of the Mountain Men and trading of wampum with the Native People up through modern times when the United States went off the Bretton Woods system in the 1970's ceasing to allow the conversion of dollars into gold, thus ushering us into the era of fiat money.

We also talked about how money is being used in today's global economy. Finally, we discussed stewardship, sharing, accountability and personal integrity.

"Our trip experiences," I stressed, "are based upon an all-for-one and one-for-all philosophy. Just think of how everyone has benefited from the generosity of others, even to the point of their own bankruptcy."

The lesson went wonderfully. The older boys agreed to close down their cookie business if the staff would keep the bankrupt kids from begging for treats. The business owners said they didn't really need the money but they were just tired of all that begging. We lingered a moment more over the bankruptcy issue and how it feels to be without money and the resultant emotions and circumstances that arise such as loss of dignity, control and choice. "The boys who are bankrupt will be counseled by staff and presented with options," I said.

After our hike, the bankrupt crowd was counseled, jobs were offered and accepted, and payroll started. That evening I was pleased to call the bankrupt young man's father in Florida to report that his son had demonstrated incredible initiative to earn money, having taken on the entire set of bus windows that day, earning $10.00. Interestingly, at the point when the boy was paid we asked if he wanted to put his money into the Bank of the Mountains or keep it himself. He chose to hold onto $1.00 and put the remainder in the bank. Throughout the rest of the trip he never went without money again nor were there any issues of begging, scalping or anyone going without.

Indeed, everyone embraced the sharing and stewardship concept, and I witnessed an increased closeness, more helping and more encouragement among all the young Mountain Men.

BUILDING YOUNG MEN: MONEY MANAGEMENT

1 Timothy 6:17. "Command those who are rich in this present world not to be arrogant nor to put their hope in wealth, which is so uncertain, but to put their hope in God, who richly provides us with everything for our enjoyment."

Life in America is blessed with incredible prosperity and opportunities to gain wealth. While wonderful, our society also has an undeniable drive based upon consumption and self-comparison—a downside that needs to be acknowledged if we want to adequately prepare our kids to deal with money. Advertising is the fuel of our economic engine that drives desire for goods and services. As new goods and services are created, advertising pushes thoughts to the forefront of our minds suggesting that, "If I could just get a better job, make more money, get this or that, or be like him or her then everything would be fine."

Of course, this is a falsehood. Nothing against ambition, as it is the marvelous elixir driving innovation and the creation of wealth. But left unchecked, the constant pursuit of better jobs, better homes, more money, more stuff, comes with a price. As we strive to pursue wealth, our lives can easily become unbalanced. If not careful, we can fall into the snares of envy and greed. Such emotions ultimately produce strife that creeps into our lives, grows over time and corrupts our sense of inner peace, our relationships and even our health.

This simply doesn't need to be the case. We have free will and can choose how we approach life and our relationship to money. In scripture, Jesus discussed money in fully twenty percent of his messages. Scriptures contain over 2,000 references regarding money. Obviously, the management of money is an important concept for people to understand. We live in a fiat based financial economy. We have faith in our government, or mostly we do. Look at how faith in the dollar can become skewed. Look at the evaluations of some current social media companies that have little to no profits. Some of these with billion plus dollar valuations are based upon a concept called monthly active users, not traditional revenue models such as price multiples. The company valuations are based on faith that these users will not only continue but will increase over time and that such users offer marketing opportunities for advertising and corollary product sales. Whatever the future portends, faith in money is not the correct place to embrace total faith. Fortunes come and fortunes go. Countries and societies come and go. God is the only true entity wherein our faith should be placed.

This is a challenge facing us as we convey lessons regarding money to our kids. If we choose to have them educated by the world, through a hands-off approach at home, then we are planning to experience significant frustrations, failures and pain along their path to adulthood. We also risk permanently losing them to the world. Studies unerringly point to disagreement over money or its mismanagement as either the number one or number two cause of relationship tension and divorce in America. This doesn't need to be the case.

Consider the Boys in Your Life....

Starting out at a young age, teach kids in a structured fashion what money is, what our financial obligations are to God, and how they should interact with others about money. These are the keys to personal responsibility and financial success in adulthood. There are many, many wonderful resources for parents to use to train kids. For instance, Larry Burkett offers leadership models in his books *Money Matters for Kids* and *Money Matters for Teens*. And for adults, there is *Debt-Free Living* and *The World's Easiest Guide to Finances*. The idea here is to take a focused and intentional step toward training yourself and your children about money and then sticking with it.

Start today. You, your boys and your family will be rewarded and God will be honored.

SOUL MEDICINE
Rock Creek, Montana 2013

"The power of laughter lies in its ability to lift the spirit."

— Bob Hope

I t was sneaky, admittedly. Several youngsters waited patiently behind the trees, one on either side of the trail leading back to camp and the Mountain Man bus. Dressed in war-paint made of ashes, chalk and red dye and grasping handmade tomahawks, they giggled uncontrollably at the unsuspecting fellow camper coming down the path. The plan was to surprise and abduct him. Other boys watched the unfolding scenario. Slowly, the happy and whistling camper came closer and closer. Just as he came abreast of the trees, the two youngsters jumped out screaming and whooping in war-like cries and dragged him down the path. The remaining campers could not resist the adventure and so ran laughing to the scene of the abduction. By the time they arrived, the victim was sitting upright next to another tree, his captors dancing around him laughing and whooping in victory.

This scenario was an example of humor, from a twelve-year-old's perspective, unleashed. While still shaken, the victim thought the surprise was one of the most unexpected of his life and pretty funny! Laughter abounded. He already knew that such antics were likely to occur on this adventure as they had happened before. Boys everywhere are alike. They love to laugh, and they love to surprise each other with light-hearted fun. Hide and Seek, Capture the Flag, game after game invented by youngsters to produce adrenaline and laughter.

Later in the trip the staff demonstrated their own version of humor. After dinner and as the fire was burning down with everyone circled around, a staff member announced he had some personal business and would return soon. No one much paid attention. This evening's campfire story was about a haunting of the area back in the 1800s. As the story unfolded, suspense began to build. The flames of the fire accented the faces of the boys, their eyes full of wonder, silently waiting for what came next. For fifteen minutes, the story unfolded, with creepy descriptions of a ghost and the haunting. When the fire was but soft, orange embers, the only light in the night, the story-teller recounted that the ghost had been seen in later times as well... as recently as last year and in this very area.

Boys stiffened. They looked at one another wondering if this could be real or was it just a story. Surely it was just a story, or was it?

The storyteller then began a slow, deliberate wind-down of the narrative pausing for several seconds when telling about some missing boys who still hadn't been found. He whispered that towns-people had reported seeing a tall and lumbering ghost with a ghoulish, monster face who had supposedly been in this exact spot the night the boys went missing.

Again, the boys looked at one another across the glowing embers. Quietly and without warning, a phantom figure appeared way back in the distance. As though an apparition, indistinct in the darkness of night, first here, then there, it began slowly moving toward the fire. Its face now becoming more distinct, a scary Frankenstein face of green complete with bloody stitches. Growling and grumbling, it grabbed a young man and dragged him away from the fire. Boys screamed! Bedlam ensued! Every boy jumped up and ran for his life!

Soon after, the ghost revealed himself as our missing staffer. He returned with the captured boy to camp, laughing and joking about the experience. Everyone resumed their places around the fire, now laughing and relaxed asking how the ghost did that. Excitement—generated by imagination, resulting in trepidation—had totally engaged the minds of these boys out in the wilds of the Montana.

Laughter truly is the best medicine for mankind. Every day has laughter so look for it!

BUILDING YOUNG MEN: HUMOR

Job 8:21. "He will yet fill your mouth with laughter and your lips with shouts of joy."

Today society often mistakes crudity for humor. Real humor is clean and produces real laughter about real-life scenarios.

A great wit of my time was Lewis Timberlake of Austin, Texas. As one of the world's top motivational speakers and trainers, he always had a story that made people laugh; this put people at ease and into a frame of mind that helped them become receptive to learning about life. One day I was at church attending his Sunday school class. His fellowship of friends in attendance that day went back in some cases over forty years. It is within this context that Lewis loosened up the class that Sunday morning. Here's what he said:

> *"I gave a talk last week in Austin as part of a group of speakers. Our hosts told us the circus was in town, and they had arranged for us to meet the members of the circus: Tom Thumb, the smallest man in the world; Sleeping Beauty, the most beautiful woman in the world, and a third player, The Ugliest Man in the World. So we all went downtown to meet the show's characters. Backstage the first person we met was Tom Thumb. Sure enough, he was so small they had to pick him up and put him on a table for us to see and talk to. Amazing.*
>
> *"The next person we met was Sleeping Beauty, the world's most beautiful woman. As we stepped behind the curtain, there she was! Beautiful was not even an expression that captured this woman's amazing beauty. She was gorgeous! Dark flowing black hair, dazzling blue eyes, she really was something!*
>
> *"The final curtain was ahead. Our hosts stopped us short saying, 'Now this next person is unusual. He is pretty hard to look at so if you don't want to meet him, I understand.' We all agreed we wanted to meet the Ugliest Man in the World so we stepped behind the curtain. Wow! This man, if it was a man, was truly ugly. I mean more than double-ugly. I don't even know how to tell you how ugly he was. Frankly, he was hideous. I gathered my wits, stepped up and introduced myself saying, 'Hello, I am Lewis Timberlake.' The man looked at me. I mean I guess he looked at me and said, 'I have heard of you.' I was flattered*

*and somewhat taken aback and said, 'Thanks.' Then
I said, 'People say you are the Ugliest Man in the
World. Is that right?' The man stopped, looked down
and then looked at me with one odd eye and said,
'That's what they say, but I have heard there is another.
Who is Tim McCoy?"*

Immediately there was a loud yell from the back of the class.
"TIMBERLAKE!" a voice called out. "I'LL SEE YOU AFTER
CLASS IN THE BACK!" The entire class instantly broke up and
roared in spontaneous laughter. You see, Tim McCoy is an old and
dear friend of Lewis and was standing at the back of the class that
day. Lewis had done it again, Tim had become yet another victim of
the Timberlake humor. By the way, Tim is a good looking man, he
was just in the wrong place at the wrong time!

If you can't laugh your way through life, life will become very,
very unpleasant not only for you, but for those around you. Look at
the cultures that don't have laughter as a major part of life; they are
often a serious, depressed and angry people. A lesson for us to learn
is to make a habit of looking for laughter and joy in life. It's soul
medicine. Once found, share your joy with one another. Try not to
take yourself so seriously: we are meant to laugh.

Consider the Boys in Your Life....

What place does joy, laughter and fun play in the life of you and
your boys? Is your home a place full of humor or is everyone given to
solemnity, or worse? Is there bickering, arguing, even yelling? Make
a point to introduce laughter into your life even if you aren't funny.
Life is often funny if you make a practice of looking for it. Boys,
and everyone for that matter, need the healing medicine of laughter
every day in their lives. Try it. Even if you fail that will be funny!

TRIUMPH

Austin, Texas, July 2003

"Great things are done when men and mountains meet."
— William Blake

T he red light blinked once, then twice, and the engineer gave us a thumbs-up through the studio window. The show was now live. Today was a Sunday afternoon and three of us were sitting before large microphones in the soundproof studio of ESPN Outdoor America's show in Austin, Texas. The youngest of our three was Dakota. Only thirteen, he had celebrated his entry into teen hood during our Mountain Men trip earlier in the summer. He looked confident as he sat before the host with the large headset on, a smile of excitement radiating from his face. The studio host welcomed listeners to the program and announced he had special guests in the studio today: Dakota and me from the Fort Smith Mountain Men Adventure Camp, just returning from a two-week expedition to Yellowstone National Park.

The host began by asking about the program. I introduced the camp as I always do, explaining that it is an adventure and learning experience for young men that teaches leadership, natural science and history... things like the westward expansion during the Mountain Men era. He was particularly interested in the Mountain Men so I explained that this era offered us an opportunity to teach young men real history in real places out west.

"On this particular trip, for example, we visited the gravesite of Sacagawea," I said. "She was the Shoshone Indian maiden who was the interpreter and who saved the Lewis and Clark expedition from certain destruction by the Indians on more than one occasion. I explained that at the gravesite, we had investigated the record carved into the headstone while gazing out across the snow-covered peaks of the Wind River Range of Wyoming. The boys were quite moved to see a grave next to hers of Jean Baptist Charbonneau, her child who was born early into the expedition, now at rest beside his mother. While there remains much debate to this day about where the actual gravesite of Sacagawea is or is not, this experience helped bring history to life.

Next our host asked Dakota, "When you got back home, what did your friends think about your adventure?" Without hesitation, he said, "They don't really get it."

"How do you mean they don't get it?" the host inquired.

Dakota explained that when he tried to tell friends about how cool it had been in the mountains with the campfires and the elk, the cool places we went, they didn't seem interested and didn't understand. "Most of my friends spent their summers playing inside on video games or watching TV." The host then understood what Dakota was trying to explain. He asked, "So what part did you enjoy most?"

"The outdoors, the food, everything was awesome!"

At this point I brought up how Dakota had been unanimously selected by the staff to be honored as the outstanding camper. "We delivered the honor at a fireside gathering at Camp Hale, Colorado, the site of alpine and winter training for the 10th Mountain Division of the United States Army during World War II," I said. "Dakota distinguished himself above all other campers through his cheerful willingness to help everyone throughout the adventure. His friendliness also made him a favorite among the campers. And he displayed exceptional leadership skills early in the camp which continued to develop throughout the trip. In fact, it was his cheerful presence that earned him the nickname, 'Smiling Chipmunk.'"

As the discussion continued, I shared with our host how I had not really prepared for our ceremony at Camp Hale as originally intended, and didn't have a suitable award for Dakota. I explained that we had enjoyed our usual recounting of the day's adventures and experiences around a campfire, including guitar entertainment by my son Ryan and others. I went on to explain that I had shared stories about the contributions the men and women of Camp Hale had made to our freedom. When the fire had slowly begun to burn down, I had told the camp it was time to announce the awards. After recognizing several young men as rising stars, we had called Dakota to stand beside me. I recounted how everyone had cheered as I reached down and pulled the scabbard off the belt I was wearing and then handed Dakota my prized Buck knife.

I recalled how his face had shown true amazement. Here Dakota had received a gift more special to him than anything I might have purchased along the way, and it was given spontaneously in the true spirit of sharing. I kept thinking how God moves in mysterious ways and had somehow sparked the idea for the knife on the way over to the campfire. Dakota was thrilled as were the other boys. I closed the fireside chat by reflecting that all the boys had achieved a major accomplishment in life through their participation in this leadership adventure. They had endured cold nights, sleeping outside for two weeks, hiking and exploring, and they had worked together to cook, clean and pack. They had learned how to get along with everyone and how to encourage one another—truly skills they would be proud of and use their entire lives.

Soon after, ESPN Outdoor America's show wrapped up and the host thanked us. Since then and that early award ceremony, my Mountain Men camp has gone on even longer adventures, some up to twenty-eight days all the way into Alaska. The results are always the same. Young men return tired, but proud and confident. They come back an inch or two taller emotionally. When they discuss their summer with friends, family and teachers, knowledge from the trips comes out and they are confident because they are speaking from first-person experiences. Not from videos, books or what someone else told them.

Today, as always, it is a pleasure to hear from former campers, now from the vantage point of young adulthood, as they continue to recount their experiences. It makes me recall the days when I was twelve and first saw the Rocky Mountains myself as a camper on the famous Meyer's Mountain Men adventure camps. How is it that these memories remain so vibrant so many years later? I believe it is because as men we are hardwired for outdoor adventures. I believe that true adventure, learning and maturity come from exploring and doing real things in the real world.

BUILDING YOUNG MEN: PRIDE OF ACCOMPLISHMENT

Philippians 4:13. "I can do everything through him who gives me strength."

Pride of accomplishment, success, positive self-esteem, confidence and achieving goals are all concepts that our society values and strives for. We know that positive self-esteem is built upon confidence and that confidence comes from step-by-step successes, which can only be gained through hard work and goal-setting. And that crucial first step—initially setting and making a commitment to goals—often cannot be accomplished alone. Boys need coaches who cheer them on. They need mom, dad, friends, family, church, school, organizations. These are the support structures that are required to produce successful young men. These support structures along with dedicated effort from the participants help lead boys to learning and eventually to a sense of accomplishment.

One thing we can do to help start this process in our kids is to help them identify their innate gifts, also thought of as abilities and passions, and their current skillsets. Such guidance will help insure they gain confidence because it will open doors to opportunities from which they can set goals and begin practicing. They can fail, recover and learn within the bounds of their safe environment with good coaching.

Proven strategies for building confidence may, catch this, *not* include an emphasis on technology. In fact, in a January 2015 article in *The New York Times* entitled "Can Students Have Too Much Tech?" Susan Pinker examines a study by Duke University economists Jacob Vigdor and Helen Ladd that shows how disadvantaged students who gained access to computers between the fifth and eighth grades actually had a persistent decline in math and reading skills over time; this remained true for as long as the researchers tracked them. Why? There is still speculation but one very good guess is these children were using computers unsupervised, simply for entertainment and not schoolwork. This study is part of a recent trend being discussed today among educators and researchers around the question, "Is it time for more low-tech?"

Technology can be extraordinarily useful and it is cool. It is not going away. But we are in the midst of a paradigm shift in our culture concerning its integration and use within society. What is needed now is a step back to look at how technology is being used in education and in our lives in general. Within education, Randy Yerrick, a professor of education at the University of Buffalo, suggests that technology's use within education is only worth the investment when it is perfectly suited to the task—for example, like simulations in science.

For years technology has been used largely under the premise of being a tool to engage students in order for them to want to learn. This engagement is primarily through entertainment and gaming. In some scenarios this may be a viable approach. Yet it has also led to student apathy because factual memorization, the lowest levels of Bloom's taxonomy of educational objectives, isn't fun or easy compared to Googling answers or playing games. The problem is that if many of our students are not achieving at even the lowest levels of Bloom's model how can we expect them to achieve at the highest levels of analysis, evaluation and creation? Stay tuned for further research and findings as we ride the ever-accelerating escalator into the information age. What we do know for sure from decades of investigation is this: if you really want to help students succeed in school and in life, the most effective helping strategies involve your being available, spending time with them and listening to them. Most important, helping kids build strong and trusting relationships—where they feel safe and willing to share openly—leads to their gaining confidence and a willingness to try, fail and recover. Ultimately then, they will feel pride of accomplishment. That's really what life is all about.

To put things another way: What people are learning the hard way is that the path of enablement leads to the road of entitlement which leads to the highway of frustration and failure when real life kicks in. As Helen Keller famously observed, "There are no shortcuts to any place worth going."

Consider the Boys in Your Life....

So try taking the high road of being available to your kids, every single day even at your inconvenience, even when you are exhausted. Make them your top priority by giving undiluted time to them. Your children and you will both be rewarded. With that in mind, consider the question, how confident are your young men? What accomplishments are you helping them achieve? Teaching personal goal-setting in areas like service, academics, sports, faith-building and outdoor adventure works! Take an inventory today of the confidence-building experiences you are providing for them. Be judicious in your choices. Today, parents are often over loading their kids with "activities." While well intended, they are driving their kids and themselves nuts with busyness because they think their kids will end up being non-competitive. Worse still, some parents are using activities as baby sitters. These approaches are social fallacies and parental shortcuts. Instead, take time to create intentional, specific opportunities that compliment your child's personality and interests, and don't overload them or yourselves. Take balanced and appropriate actions and then watch what develops! You will be amazed at how your child will bloom.

Epilogue: We Are the Builders

These stories about young Mountain Men have hopefully inspired you to undertake adventures of your own with the young men in your life. Consider now, this poem which brilliantly illuminates our challenge to be leaders of youth.

The Builders

James Albert Spear, 1944

All things living are prone to have dreams,
And each one are builders it seems,
The ants or the beaver or birds on the wing,
Each one is busy building their nest in the spring.
They are builders.

The architect plans, then the carpenters come,
And in a short time have erected a home,
The painter, the landscaper, each has a part
In completing the home so dear to our heart.
They are builders.

But the greatest of structures we ever know
Is character building – its completion is slow
As we are the architect and carpenter, too,
And we alone all the labor must do.
We are builders.

A foundation of truthfulness, an honesty wall,
A desire to be helpful to those who may fall,
Work every day just as hard as you can
In building the character desired in the man.
You are the builder.

INDEX OF SCRIPTURAL CITATIONS

Acknowledgements

L ife is an amazing adventure. As we, mere humans, wind our way through life's trails, we are subject daily to the rhythms of physical capabilities, social circumstances, emotions, choices and decisions. And so many opportunities! The reason everyone wants to come to America is virtually limitless opportunity. For me, yet another opportunity on my trail has arrived as I am able to present this book. To extend a mere thanks, for the unbelievable learning and growth I have gained through the unselfish support and guidance from world-class leaders, family and friends, seems trite and ineffectual. For without their help and encouragement, this book would never have come to be.

I wish to thank Bob Meyer, "The Austin Mountain Man," a visionary leader of youth and men since the 1950's and one of my key inspirations since age twelve. He is one of the most positive, optimistic and enjoyable characters of my life. Bob's insights into boys, his humor, wisdom, guidance and encouragement made all the difference in the lives of thousands of Mountain Men and their families. Thanks Bob!

To Robby Robertson of the famed Camp Longhorn, thanks! Without your support, the Fort Smith Mountain Men would not be! To my beautiful, wise and witty wife, Rhonda, a person whose gifts of insight, commitment to truth, pursuit of family and of helping others is nothing short of amazing, thank you sweetheart! And to my fabulous and loyal family, I appreciate the individual and collective experiences that have made my life rich, full and complete. Together, our faith in God has led to a closeness that is inexplicable and that vibrates with each moment we spend together. Thank you for loving me and supporting me.

To my favorite leadership teacher Lewis Timberlake, who was my little-league baseball coach, Sunday school teacher, renowned motivational speaker, author and friend, thank you Lewis! To Don Rude, my dear friend and hiking buddy along the trails of life, a gifted author, encourager and leader with incredible insights, thank you for all you do to make my life and the lives of those you serve so very rich. To Dr. Gene Davenport, my dear friend, mentor and hunting buddy, a man of character and selfless service at the highest levels of accomplishment, thank you for your friendship and role modeling. To Mark Caddell, a friend who caught my vision and through encouragement helped me create reality, thank you! To Nicholas Cowey, a gifted man with wide-ranging knowledge and a great sense of humor, you inspire me and kids everywhere, thank you pal! To the talented Elinor Griffith, whose time, interest and skills in editing offer readers something worthy of their time, thank you for the experiences and the friendship!

Finally, it is with deep affection and respect that I extend my sincere thanks to all of the Mountain Men, past and present. Guys who come from all walks of life, from all over the country and as far away as Canada and England, guys who teach me much more than I ever teach them, thank you for the adventures.... and may God bless each of you and yours.

Ron Smith

About the Author

R on Smith is a Christian layman who lives in the Texas Hill country just outside of Austin with his childhood sweetheart and wife Rhonda. Following a successful career in the high-tech industry, he is now a middle school science teacher, camp owner and life coach. He is co-author with Don Rude of *Simple Man, Simple Prayer* (CrossBooks, 2014) *(*www.simpleman.org), a leadership guide for men. Ron's passion is to help people identify positive life directions and choices through teaching, his life coaching practice, and his youth camp, San Gabriel Outdoor Adventures, (sgoadventures.com).

CPSIA information can be obtained
at www.ICGtesting.com
Printed in the USA
FSOW02n1932260615
8324FS